MW00778450

THE VIRGIN MARY

IN

THE MARONITE CHURCH

Bishop Boutros Gemayel

The Institute of
Bishop Boutros Gemayel
Second Edition
Beirut 2007

Translated by
Rev. Georges Y. El-Khalli, Ph.D.

Printed in the United States of America

E.T. NEDDER Publishing
c/o Theological Book Service
7313 Mayflower Park Drive
Zionsville, IN 46077

Front Cover Design:
The Virgin Mary According to the Maronite Tradition
Ileej, Tenth Century.

Back Cover Design:
The Virgin Mary as adapted from the
Icon Studio of the Maronite Eparchy of Cyprus
and inspired from the Virgin Mary
of the Rabbula Gospel, 586 A.D.

Additional copies of this publication may be purchased be sending
Check or money order for (in U.S.) $15 plus shipping and handling to E.T.
NEDDER Publishing c/o Theological Book Service, 7313 Mayflower Park Drive
Zionsville, IN 46077. Or call toll free 1-888-247-3023
Order Number 7615

ISBN: 978-1-893757-61-5

DEDICATION

The Blessed Virgin Mariam, "Our Lady of the Assumption" in Chebanieh, Maten, Lebanon, is the patroness of my hometown. It is to Mariam, the Mother of God, that I owe the first and the greatest gratitude for the translation of this book. Her guidance led me to it; her wisdom inspired me to translate it; her intercession invigorated me when I lacked enthusiasm and her protection inspirited me to complete it.

To my Parents Youssef and Mariam, whose love brought me into the world and afforded me the Catholic Faith. Youssef infused within me the Maronite Syriac Tradition as soon as I opened my eyes to life and Mariam initiated me with the love of Our Mother, the Blessed Virgin Mariam. Youssef, who is now with the Lord, pleads for me and sustains my priestly vocation; Mariam, with her daily rosaries and prayers, supports my ministry.

CONTENTS

ACKNOWLEDGMENTS

For a priest who is ministering full time to an active parish, it is very difficult to find free time, especially when undertaking a translation of this magnitude. Such a project requires concentration, determination and dedication. Thanks to the kindness, assistance, advice, generosity and support of several individuals who have been instrumental in helping me accomplish my goal. I would like to express to each one of them my heartfelt gratitude and deepest appreciation:

His Excellency Boutros Gemayel, bishop of the Maronite Eparchy of Cyprus, who graciously granted me the official copyright permission in order to translate his personal work into English.

His Excellency Gregory J. Mansour, bishop of the Eparchy of St. Maron, Brooklyn, who approved the publication of this translated work with his Eparchial Seal. It is through his continued support and blessing that this work came to fruition. I will forever admire his fervent zeal and treasure his genuine friendship.

Chorbishop Seely Beggiani, who reviewed the doctrinal content, reading the final draft and giving his invaluable comments. I owe him a debt of thanks for his constructive advice and encouragement.

Sister Mary Anita Benecki, C.S.S.F., who proofread and edited the work, placing the final touches at the end of my two-year journey with the Blessed Virgin Mary.

Mr. Elias Attea Jr. who provided generous financial support in making the printing project of this book a reality.

Mr. Ernest T. Nedder and Mr. Kamal F. Jowdy who provided their publishing and printing expertise.

FOREWARD

To the English Edition 2008

Father Georges El-Khalli, Pastor of St John Maron Parish in Williamsville, New York and Director of the Office of Catechesis in the Eparchy of St Maron, has done a great favor to Maronites and friends in the English-speaking world. He has translated the scholarly work of His Excellency Boutros Gemayel, Maronite Bishop of Cyprus, which was commissioned for the 1988 Marian Year and published under the title *The Virgin Mary in the Maronite Church*. To this date it is the definitive work on Mary for Maronite Catholics.

As His Excellency Youssef Beshara, Bishop of Antelias, Lebanon who commissioned the work wrote, "It may be fairly easy for an average Catholic to refer to Marian Dogma...However, it is not easy for a Maronite to find what may quench his spiritual thirst and nourish his piety from the richness of the Maronite Church's devotion to Mary." Bishop Gemayel's text does precisely that.

It is our hope that in these pages the reader will encounter once again, and time and time again, the Virgin Mary, as seen through the lens of the Maronite Church. A Maronite image of Mary is complete in Catholic dogma and true to all references of her from the Sacred Scriptures. By means of the Maronite Liturgy and the Church's devotions to her, Mary becomes once again our spiritual companion and guide. But most of all she becomes once again for us "mother", as she was to John when Jesus gave her to his care at the foot of the Cross.

There is no greater gift for an author or translator than that of a grateful reader. I am such a reader who has come away from this experience with a greater appreciation and love for Mary from Scripture and Tradition as beautifully woven together in Maronite prayer and devotion. Bishop Gemayel covers the early Church Fathers, the Councils of the Church, St. Ephrem, Maronite prayer and devotion, and with the help of Father El Khalli, has bequeathed to us a spiritual treasure just waiting to be discovered.

Even before the great pronouncement of the Council of Nicaea, St. Ephrem, and now along with him all who will read and benefit from this great work, proclaimed: "my bones will cry out from the grave, Mary is the Mother of God."

+ Gregory John Mansour
Eparch of St. Maron of Brooklyn
April 7, 2008

PREFACE

To the English Edition 2008

Because of persecutions, migration has become a phenomenon which accompanied the Maronites since their inception and the Monastery of Saint Maron on the Orontes River. They abandoned the vicinity of Antioch (Antakiat, a city in southern Turkey today) to find a safe haven in the rugged mountains of Lebanon as early as the sixth century. Invasions persisted through the Umayyad, the Fatimide and the Mamlouk dynasties and continued through the Ottoman Empire. The last two centuries were not any more forgiving to Lebanon and the Maronites. The massacres of the 1840s and 1860s, the two World Wars and the 1975 Lebanese civil war kept alive the migration phenomenon. Oppression, famine, strife, lack of job opportunities and other types of hardship forced many Maronites to migrate again, not only to nearby Middle Eastern countries, but to the West such as Europe, the Americas and Oceania.

In the New World, they have established communities and built churches to preserve their heritage and to maintain their spiritual tradition. It seemed, at the time, that the United States of America was the most attractive country for job opportunity and freedom. A Doctoral dissertation entitled, "The Role of Education in the Assimilation Process of Lebanese in the United States" claims that the Maronites have lived in America for four generations. [1] At the present time, we are well into the fifth generation of American born Maronites. The newly founded exarchate in 1966 soon became the Diocese of Saint Maron, U.S.A. which covered the entire American

---

[1] Georges Y. El-Khalli, *The Role of Education in the Assimilation Process of Lebanese in the United States*, the University of Southern California, 1990. The research consists of a survey questionnaires and interviews conducted in five American cities, stretching from Boston to Los Angeles.

landscape. Due to the increase of migration, the influx of Maronites during the recent Lebanese civil war and the establishment of new parishes throughout the country, this Jurisdiction developed into two Eparchies totally separate and independent in 1994. The Eparchy of Saint Maron of Brooklyn, New York, serves all the states that touch the Eastern Seaboard, while the Eparchy of Our Lady of Lebanon of Los Angeles covers the rest of the country.

This recent Jurisdiction brought Maronites closer and helped them reclaim their spiritual identity. In spite of the fact that they live in a secular world, far removed from their Middle Eastern culture, American born Maronites preserved their religious heritage, lived their faith and spirituality they had inherited from their forebears. Many a liturgical service did not appeal to them unless it was translated into the vernacular, but they still adhered. For example: They would participate in paraliturgical services such as the Benediction with the Icon of the Virgin Mary, they would proudly chant the popular hymn of *"Ya Umm Allah"* which means "O Mother of God," but something is still missing. What is this devotion all about? Where does it come from? What does it mean and why the blessing with the Icon is of such deep spiritual significance? They have not experienced such devotions in the churches of their friends. They feel proud, unique and special, yet they are thirsty to learn and anxious to delve deeper into their rich spiritual heritage. Both Maronite Eparchies in the United States are not sparing any efforts to keep the faithful in the fold and to hand on intact the faith and the tradition.

Ministering to the Maronite Church in America for almost three decades, serving the Eparchy in various capacities and presently as the Eparchial Director of Religious Education, we sense a dire need to catechize young generations, born in the United States, about the hidden treasures of the Maronite spirituality. The chief purpose of this translation is to make available to them the origins of Marian devotions and the main reasons why these paraliturgical services are so embedded in their culture, liturgies and rituals! It is crucial to introduce to them this spiritual heritage, generation by generation, so they may know where the attachment of their parents to Mary comes from and, more importantly, that they may possess the proper reasons to be proud of it.

After brushing off the dust of the stratified centuries from the layers of the Icon of the Virgin Mary and revealing her true face through the Maronite Tradition, we hope that this translated work would be of benefit to any interested reader. Also we hope that it would relate more effectively to the younger generation and explain to them why our ancestors, during centuries of persecution, have chosen to veil themselves with the mantle of the Blessed Mother and still, to this day, fly to her protection.

Another purpose for this translation is to bring to our friends, from various Christian backgrounds, the authentic image of the Virgin Mary, which was drawn by the Church, shaped by its Ecumenical Councils and beautifully painted by the Maronite Syriac Tradition. May it help mirror the importance of the Virgin Mary in the life of the Church as it is fully expressed and as it has been lived for centuries by the Maronites. It would be gratifying if our work has somewhat helped the reader understand why the Maronite have such commitment and love for the Virgin Mary.

Finally, we hope that this translation prompts and inspires other translations of relevant research so that Maronites, in the United States as well as in all Western countries, may continue to grow and, at the same time, remain attached to their spiritual roots and rich Tradition. It is also hoped that more Maronite scholars living in the West publish new research about their Tradition, enrich Western libraries with Eastern resources and reveal hidden spiritual treasure to Christians living in the West.

Rev. Georges Y. El-Khalli, Ph.D.,
Pastor of Saint John Maron Church
Director of Religious Education:
Eparchy of Saint Maron of Brooklyn.

September 8, 2007
Nativity of the Blessed Virgin Mary

INTRODUCTION
TO EDITION 1988

After the opening of the Marian year, a committee was formed in the Maronite Eparchy of Cyprus to make available to all faithful the benefits of the jubilee year. The committee thought it necessary to seize the opportunity to strengthen the veneration of the Virgin Mary, not only through spiritual festivities, but specifically by introducing the faithful to the true face of Mary and its unique role through the teaching of the Church. Since Church teachings are manifested in worship and dogma, the committee suggested to publish two books: the first would be brief about the Marian Dogma, the second about Mary in the Maronite Church.

It may be fairly easy for an average Catholic to refer to the Marian Dogma especially in the encyclical by the Holy Father "Redemptoris Mater" or in English, "Mother of the Redeemer," and the teachings of the Council of Vatican II "Dogmatic Constitution in the Church, chapter 8." However, it is not easy for a Maronite to find what may quench his spiritual thirst, nourish his piety and prove the strength of his veneration to Mary and the richness of his Marian tradition, due to the scarcity of research in this field. What is really troubling is that foreign devotions have overwhelmed this tradition, most often nourishing the faithful superficial spiritual emotion, leading them to exaggeration and extremism and veiling the true reality of the face of Mary.

Therefore, we felt it necessary to publish a book about the Virgin Mary in which the view of the Maronite Church will be clarified through a theological and practical understanding, especially in various liturgical devotions.

Who is more capable of undertaking such a challenge than Monsignor Boutros Gemayel, the Vicar General of our Eparchy, who volunteered to face such a monumental project—a dream he always wished to concretize. I have assigned him this task because it requires delicate research and expedient completion, since he has a long history of practice in this field and possesses great potentials in liturgical studies coupled with a highly respected ecclesial degree and a wide pastoral experience in numerous fields.

This book discusses the role of Mary from the standpoint of the life of a particularly defined Church—a role in relation to her Son and in the life of the Church. There are certain characteristics of Mary in this Church which were carried through by the prayers of the Maronites, by their liturgical practices and diversified devotions. If it is true that prayer, liturgical prayer in particular, is the true expression of faith, then, through their theological understanding of the role of Mary, the Maronites possess special characteristics dating back to the origins of the Dogma which radiate the texts of the Scriptures, the teaching of the Fathers and the deep simplicity of the individual faithful. These characteristics do not separate Mary from the life of her Son nor do they separate her from the life of the faithful. For being the Mother of God, Mary is a compassionate mother for us who accompanies us throughout the stages of life. Her divine motherhood, through which she surpassed all creatures, is a generous source granting graces to all those who honor her so that she may lead them to her Son.

Therefore, it is necessary for us to go back to these sources and delve into our ecclesiastical heritage! Doing so in true faith, we may invigorate our veneration to Mary and our filial attachment will lead us to imitate her virtues and emulate her strong faith which was for her a journey of life based on the love of God. Our attachment to Mary is the attachment of children to a mother who had, and must continue to have, a shrine and an altar in each and every town, an icon and a place in each and every home, veneration and respect in each and every heart.

We hope that this book, during this Marian year, revives our love to Mary based on our understanding of her unique role in our salvific history and in the history of our Maronite Tradition.

As the author strives through his book to reach this goal, may the Virgin Mary generously reward him. With personal regards along with the Marian Committee in the Eparchy of Cyprus, we offer him our best wishes and gratitude.

Qornet Shahwan, April 19, 1988

> \+ Youssef Bishara
> Bishop of the Maronite
> Eparchy of Cyprus

INTRODUCTION
TO EDITION 2007

The Virgin Mary
In the Maronite Church

I was born in Ain El-Kharroubeh, near the Church of Our Lady of Perpetual Help and her picture was imprinted in my eyes as soon as I saw the light. At her baptismal font I have put on Christ, with her Chrism I was confirmed, in her church and on its steps I knelt and prayed and on her lectern I shared in the singing of Syriac hymns. Countless times I carried incense and candles and brought flowers to honor her. On her altar I celebrated my first *Qurbono* and many other *Qurboneh* since I became a pastor. When I was appointed to shepherd the Maronite Church in Cyprus, Our Lady of Perpetual Help was there in Nicosia waiting for me in my Cathedral. It is in the light of this life-journey that I present this book.

The Virgin Mary is our companion on the journey who is vigilant and patient. She is the one about whom the Son said from the Cross "behold your mother." She gave us Christ, so what can we say? The mother of Christ is our mother and the mother of Christ is the mother of the Church. The church that has no place for the Virgin Mary is not a church.

The Virgin Mary was with Christ and for Christ at all times: from the announcement of the Angel in Nazareth, to the manger in Bethlehem, to the Temple, to Cana, to the Cross, to the event of Golgotha which shook the entire universe, to the darkness of the tomb, to the bright light of the Resurrection, to the storm of

Pentecost—the Virgin Mary was there standing and repeating "Do whatever he tells you."

Our Maronite Church is apostolic and Marian; it was built upon the Apostles and the love of the Virgin Mary. Hers is a long journey with the Virgin Mary whose icon is engraved in every heart and honored in every home. Every morning and every evening and with every difficulty, the sigh of "Ya 'Adra," which is rendered "O Blessed Virgin," comes out naturally. In every dwelling place and with every travel, the Icon of the Virgin Mary is the constant companion.

Through this book, I have intended to introduce people to the way we honor the Virgin Mary in our Maronite Church. Also I have wished to show the theological richness which emanates from the liturgical ceremonies and texts, and to point out the graces that we may receive when we honor the Mother who loves us and whom we love.

I am delighted to see that some people are benefiting from what this book has to offer. I am most grateful in having been faithful in my love for the Virgin Mary throughout both my priestly and Episcopal journeys.

I would like to conclude where I have actually started: I thank you, my dear Mother because, by serving your altar, I have received the faith and learned prayer and the Scriptures; and by participating at your lectern, I have grown to love the rituals. I thank you, my dear Mother, because you have alleviated the burden of my Episcopal ministry on the altar of your Cathedral.

Here I am today, as I complete the cycle from Our Lady of Perpetual Help in Ain El-Kharroubeh, Lebanon, to Our Lady of Perpetual Help in Cyprus, I bring my book as a bouquet of roses offering it to you as a token of a child's love to his mother.

Ain El-Kharroubeh, August 5, 2007

+ Bishop Boutros Gemayel
Maronite Bishop of Cyprus
Patriarchal Liturgical Commission

CHAPTER I

Mary and the Maronite Tradition

A journey of research about the Virgin Mary through the perception of the Maronite Church requires us to discuss the history of this church from its inception until today in order to better understand Marian thoughts in light of the historical junctures through which this church has passed. Naturally, we are not about to rewrite the whole "Maronite History" in these few short pages because historical sciences require precise exigencies and serious documentations. We are only trying to simplify the situation so the reader may be able to follow the progress of the Maronite Marian theology through various Maronite historical periods. They can be limited to five, the number of fingers on one hand, which Maronites use when they make the "sign of the Cross."

1. **The Period of Evangelization**
   The Maronites were evangelized by the Apostles in the region of Antioch and its environs. This great area developed later to become the territory of the Patriarchate of Antioch, which extended from the shores of the city of Tyre to the mountains of Lebanon and stretched out to the mountains of Cyrrhus.

2. **The Period of Education**
   The main Maronite Book is the Sacred Scripture in both of its Testaments, but in Syriac, or a translated version of it.

3. **The Period of the Early Ecumenical Councils**
   The Maronites were nourished spiritually by the faith that was chiefly based on the early ecumenical councils which had shaped, in a special way, the map of the Christian East.

4. **The Monastery of Saint Maron**

   This monastery provided the monastic spirituality of Saint Maron and his disciples; it later served as a religious center and a patriarchal residence.

5. **The See of Peter in Rome**

   The relation of the Maronites with Rome dates back to the very beginning and is still ongoing.

In light of these five combined historical junctures, we shall identify the characteristics of the Maronite Tradition through which we will be able to see the "Maronite" face of Mary.

1. The Period of Evangelization (Antioch)

The Maronite Church emerged with Saint Maron and the Monastery of Saint Maron in the fifth century, but "Maronite Christianity," i.e., Christians who became Maronites, existed prior to this date. They are the Christians of the Church of Antioch who received the Good News from the apostles and from the head of the apostles himself. Antioch is the original Church, the "city of God," in which they were first called "Christians."

The Christians of the patriarchate of Antioch were divided after the fourth ecumenical council, which is the Council of Chalcedon in 451. Some have supported the Council while others opposed it. The Maronites were among the supporters of the Council who were called "Chalcedonians."

When the Maronite Patriarchate was established in the seventh century, the Patriarch assumed the "Antiochene" title. He did not consider himself the head of a Christian sect that is rebellious or a breed that has no origins, but rather a patriarch who links the chain of the patriarchs of Antioch which practically began with Peter and Ignatius. He always added the name "Peter" to his name up until today. The diptych of the Maronite Patriarch in the Mass never began with Saint John Maron, the first Maronite patriarch, but with Peter, Ignatius and their successors.

Therefore, the Maronites continued the Antiochene Tradition; they were called as such based on their original center, the Monastery of Saint Maron. But theirs is the Antiochene theological tradition along with the school of Ephrem, James of Sarug and John Chrysostom "whose connection with Maron is through friendship" as mentioned in his letter to Maron; theirs is the Antiochene School which was headed by Theodoret who spoke of Maron as a special saint who belongs to the diocese of Cyrrhus, which is a part of Antioch. This Theodoret is one of the most influential and staunch supporters of the Council of Chalcedon.

The Antioch of Maron the hermit was also the Antioch of Maron's disciples who lived in the Monastery of Saint Maron which was called "Beit Maroun" or the house of Maron. This "Beit Maroun" became the leading Monastery in Syria II to defend the dogma of the Chalcedonian Antiochene Church. It is at this juncture when the Maronites moved from the Antioch of Maron and "Beit Maroun" to the Maronite Chalcedonian movement and then to Saint John Maron, the first patriarch, who assumed, along with his successors, the title of the "Patriarch of Antioch" and transferred it to Mount Lebanon. The early inscriptions about the Maronite Patriarch as recorded in the Gospel of Rabbula since the twelfth century is as follows: "I Peter, the patriarch, who sits on the Chair of Antioch..."[1] Said somewhat differently, as it was noted in one of the manuscripts written in Hadcheet in 1357: "In the days of Youhanna, Patriarch of Antioch, Mount Lebanon and the sea shores..."[2].

This Maronite Antioch was also in Mount Lebanon because it was neither the political nor the authoritative city, but Antioch the "city of God" and the school of councils, the Antioch of hermits and cenobites who were widespread on the mountain side, or abiding in caves and grottos. It is Antioch "the Spirit" that extended to "Mount Lebanon and the sea shores;" it is the school of faith which is filled with the preaching of the apostles and the teachings of the Church Fathers through which the Maronites were inspired both intellectually and historically.

---

[1] Boutros Daou. *Maronite Ecclesiastical Iconography, the Gospel of Rabbula and its Icons,* 1987, (p. 370).
[2] Estephan Al-Douwayhi, *The Succession of Patriarchs,* Shartouni Publisher, 1902, (p. 28).

2. The Period of Education

The Sacred Scriptures, in Syriac, in its Old and New Testaments.

The Maronite Tradition is in love with the Scripture which is in the Aramaic-Syriac language. The Old Testament is preserved with all its Books and is detailed verse by verse: The Torah, the Prophets and the rest of the Books, all of which the Maronite Tradition received either through the "Old Syriac" translation or the "Simple" (Peshitta) one. The Old Testament was read in churches and monasteries, day and night, to the point where "the eyes of the Fathers have dimmed" from revising and rectifying. However, the Maronite Tradition was first introduced to the New Testament through the "Ancient" translation more than any other. For them it has become the norm and the way of life. Quite often they would return to each verse and refer to each explanation. Scripture was amalgamated into the writings and the prayers of the Fathers. It was read daily with commentary and explanation along with prayers and chants, as it was noted in the book of *Reesh Qurian*.[3]

It is through this lively book that the face of the Virgin Mary appeared in the Maronite Tradition. A second Eve appeared to crush the head of the serpent and to restore us to the life that was lost. The "Virgin" Mary has appeared, just as the term *olmo* of the Prophet Isaiah was translated from Syriac, the virgin who will conceive and give birth to a Son who will be called Emmanuel.

In the New Testament appears the icon of the Blessed Virgin who accepts the Annunciation to become the Mother of the Word Incarnate, and who accompanies Jesus throughout the journey of Evangelization, from the cradle, to Cana, Golgotha, the Mount of Ascension, the Upper Room and to the Johannine Revelation where "a woman clothed with the sun, the moon under her feet, and on her head a crown of twelve stars." If you do not know the Sacred Scriptures, you will not meet the face of Mary in the Maronite Tradition.

---

[3] *Reesh Qurian* or in Aramaic *"Foorish Qurian"* is a collection of readings selected from the Scriptures according to the Maronite Syriac liturgical year. This book was published in Quzhayah Press in 1841. Father Youhanna Tabit published an *Ancient Maronite Reesh Qurian (1242),* Kaslik, 1988.

3. The Period of the Early Ecumenical Councils

The Maronite Tradition is the daughter of the School of Antioch which is known to the early ecumenical and other holy Councils: Nicaea, Constantinople, Ephesus and Chaldedon. It is from these four bases that the constitution of the faith was born.

In the constitution of the faith, i.e., the Creed, there is a clear teaching about Jesus Christ, the Son of God and the Son of Mary, "who took flesh from the Holy Spirit and from the Virgin Mary:"

> "We believe in one God ... in one Lord Jesus Christ the only Son of God ... eternally begotten of the Father... God from God, light from light, true God from true God..." This is the faith of the Fathers, the holy apostles, "as was defined in the Councils of Nicaea and Constantinople." Thus, Ephrem and his disciples portrayed the divine nature of Christ, against all "Alexandrian" and Arian heresies, in all of their poetry and rituals.

This is what a Maronite breathes at each offering of incense and prayer! at each candle and Eucharist! Every time his mouth opens to speak, he proclaims "true God from true God." "By the power of the Holy Spirit he was born of the Virgin Mary." The proclamation of the Fathers in Ephesus "O Mother of God" is his daily hymn with every sunrise and sunset. Is there any other title besides this one for Her? Was the Maronite Tradition ever different from what John was in the Gospel or his successors in Ephesus!

The Maronite Tradition is Nicaean in seal and essence, Ephesian in proclamation and hymns, Chalcedonian in dogma and witness! Therefore, it was a witness and a martyr for Chalcedon—Christ God and Man—two natures and one person in Christ! Such was the teaching of Leo at Chalcedon and as such professed the Maronites. This is how the Maronite Church lived! Many of her children were slaughtered like sheep and died as martyrs for the sake of Chalcedon! The Monastery of Saint Maron and its disciples are witnesses to that.

4. The Monastery of Saint Maron

The leading Monastery among the Monasteries of Syria II

Quoting previous historians, Aboul-Fida (1273-1331) states that "the Byzantine Emperor Marcian built the Monastery of Saint Maron during the second year of his reign" which means around 452 A.D. Aboul-Fida adds that "during the reign of this Emperor, Nestorius was cursed and exiled." The consensus of historians was that the disciples of Saint Maron who fought over the relic of his skull, first built a small church bearing his name and lived around it. Shortly thereafter a monastery was built on the same site which developed to be a great learning center out of which the Maronite Church had its beginning.[4]

The Maronite Tradition that stemmed from the Monastery of Saint Maron is a "Chalcedonian" movement. It was not simply a monastic movement, but from the start a "defending citadel of the faith which was professed by the early Councils," the last of which is the Council of Chalcedon. From the beginning the Maronites were known as the "grapevine of Leo." The "Melkites," however, were the followers of the king or the "Byzantine Emperor." All the emperors promoted this monastery: they built it with "Marcian," expanded it with "Justinian" and glorified it with "Heraclius." From its inception, it was never a simple isolated monastery, but the central and leading monastery in "Syria II." This claim is corroborated by the signature of the abbot, in a letter to the Fathers of the fifth ecumenical council that was held in Constantinople in 536 stating: "Paul, through the grace of God, apocrisary and delegate, for the monastery of blessed Maron, the presiding monastery over all the monasteries in Syria II, the representative of all abbots and monks of the above mentioned region."

Further, as noted in the signature of a letter to emperor Justinian in condemning the Monophysite heresy it reads: "Paul, through the grace of God, monk and delegate of the monastery of blessed Maron, the monastery which governs all the monasteries of Syria II, the spokesman of all abbots and monks of Syria II."[5]

---

4 Paul Naaman, *Theodoret of Cyrrhus and the Monastery of St. Maron*, Kaslik, 1971.
5 Peter Dib, *The Maronite Church*, I, 1930, (pp. 42-45).

This widespread Maronite movement in Syria II was the leading ecumenical Christian Catholic Antiochene theological thought which was connected with Rome and Byzantium. Since its inception, the Maronite Tradition was never a movement of simple partnership between "peasants and landlords," but rather a popular ecclesial movement headed by struggling Fathers who "shed precious tears for our salvation." They defended their movement which resulted in the struggle, even through martyrdom, for the sake of the Council of Chalcedon. This defense was evidenced by the martyrdom of the three hundred fifty Maronites in 517 as they were on a pilgrimage to the Monastery of Saint Simon the Stylite. They sent a letter to the Pope with two messengers to plead their struggle and the martyrdom of their companions in which they wrote:

"To the all blessed Hormisdas, Patriarch of the entire world, who sits on the Chair of Peter, prince of the Apostles... When Christ was in the flesh, He appointed you the leader of the shepherds, it behooves us to describe to you our sufferings and make you well aware of the wolves that are tearing apart the flock of Christ... Here is some of who they are: Severus and Peter who were never considered a part of the Christian community, for they openly, every day, condemn the holy Council of Chalcedon and our Father, the most holy, Pope Leo... who spared us immeasurable sufferings because we were being forced to ridicule this Council... As we were on a pilgrimage to the monastery of Saint Simon, the thugs had ambushed and massacred three hundred fifty men and badly wounded many others. Even those who attempted to take refuge in churches they were not spared. They burnt the monasteries..., they ransacked the churches... Do not abandon us, O most Holy Father..., as the daily attacks of these cruel monsters inflict on us irreparable wounds. We wish to inform your guardian angel that, through our deliverance, we will excommunicate all those who are condemned and excommunicated by your Apostolic See like Nestorius, Eutyches and Dioscorus..."[6]

If more details were provided about this era of Maronite history, it is only to prove that the Maronite Church is an Antiochene Christian community, following in the footsteps of the teachings of the ecumenical councils. This also shows that from the beginning the

---

[6] Peter Dib, *The Maronite Church*, I, 1930, (pp. 42-45).

Maronite Church is carrying the banner of the Virgin, the "Mother of Jesus Christ our Savior, one person in two natures." The veneration of this Church to the Virgin Mary is not just a façade; it stems from the depth of the heart and from the ancient apostolic faith that has always adopted the ecumenical councils and accepted the primacy of Peter. This is why the fifth and final base of the Maronite Tradition is: "the Faith of Peter is our Faith."

5. The See of Peter in Rome

The fidelity of the Maronites to the See of Peter in Rome did not emerge in the past few centuries, nor did it arrive with western missionaries nor imported before or after the Crusades. It is rather apostolic and Antiochene, stemming from the original roots of Christianity and developing with the teachings of the Church through its ecumenical councils. The first period is Petrine and Antiochene up to the time of Ephesus; the second is Leontine leading up to the baptism by name: "the Grapevine of Leo;" the third is the baptism by blood, "the martyrdom of the three hundred fifty" and many others. The Letter of the Maronites to Pope Hormisdas in 517 is but a "witness of faith written in blood," and the Pope's answer in 518 is but a "confirmation to their martyrdom."

The Maronites kept this relation with the Apostolic See as much as they possibly could. The last communication possible before the Islamic conquest was with Pope Honorius I (625-638), on the eve of the conquest. It is possible that the teachings of Honorius spread in the East through Emperor Heraclius by means of his "Referendum" of 634. But the Arab Islamic conquest in 636 and the interruption of communication between East and West, disrupted the Maronites from continuing their normal relations with the western world.

During exceptional and imposing circumstances the Maronite Patriarchate presided over a very dignified Apostolic Church—whose walls were torn down through unforgiving centuries which reduced it practically to a stranded Christianity, on a journey through the desert, bearing the wounds of persecution—the Church of Antioch.

With the rise of the Crusades in Antioch, the Maronites opened up new contacts with the West and started again to send messengers to the Pope until Patriarch Jeremiah Al-Amsheety was able to go to Rome, in person, in 1215 to participate in the Fourth Lateran Council. Communication with Rome was reestablished from that time on and are still ongoing. Later centuries served to strengthen these ties through the establishment of the Maronite College in Rome in 1584, through the Synod of Lebanon that was convoked in 1736, headed by the papal delegate, who was a Maronite, and through everything else that has already come and will come from Rome to our present time. The proclamation was then and still is today: "Our Faith is the Faith of Peter and the Faith of Peter is our Faith."

Through the influence of this "Roman" faith, as well as by means of the students of the Maronite College in Rome and the presence of Roman missionaries among Maronites, western Marian devotions found their way in, side by side with original Maronite Marian devotions and they were the best of companions in times of difficulties. This is but a proof to show the love of the Maronites for the Virgin Mary, Queen of both the East and the West, and the Mother of all.

Therefore, in this last period, liturgical and paraliturgical services have experienced a special type of mix of western Marian devotions with eastern ones, making the Maronites today possess a universal and comprehensive Marian devotion, which at times, with its western nature, preserved the tradition of the people of the land!

Conclusion

The Sacred Scriptures, the Church of Antioch, the Ecumenical Councils, the Monastery of Saint Maron and the See of Peter: These are the five Maronite bases which have afforded us what we have today and what our Church, which spreads from East to West, lives on. It may well be possible that her children who live in the West today outnumber those who live in the East. Therefore, today's situation of the Maronite Church differs tremendously from the time she lived in the plains of Syria or in the remote mountains of Lebanon. It has spread from Lebanon to the islands, to the plains, to Africa and Europe, especially to North, Central and South America, to Australia and Oceania and to the farthest ends of the earth.

Wherever a Maronite home happens to be, the hymn of *"Ya Umm Allah"* which means "O Mother of God" still resounds in it, whether openly or "covertly," along with the supplications of history, which is mixed with pain, tears, blood and the catastrophes of time.

CHAPTER II

Mary in the Sacred Scriptures
According to the Maronite Tradition

The foundation of religious thought and the base of the Christian doctrine is the Sacred Scriptures as received through the Church. The Book in itself is the testament of the Church, who accepted and handed it to the present Christian community. The Church in turn receives it, recites it, meditates on it and draws from its teaching and direction. Early on in various Churches designated communities were assigned to read the Sacred Books in the Church according to feast days and memorials. In the Maronite Church, each feast has its chosen readings, taken from the various Books of both the Old and the New Testaments. Designated readings were collected into a book called *Reesh Qurian*, to be more specific *Foorish Qurian,* which constitutes the "chosen readings" from the Old and the New Testaments encompassing all the feasts of the year.[7]

Referring to these chosen readings for the feasts of the Virgin Mary, we have discovered what might be called "Mary in the Sacred Scriptures according to the Maronite Tradition." We do not mean the tradition which is recorded and is only limited to doctrinal books. But we mean the living tradition that labeled the inherited Maronite centuries and marked the souls of the Maronite people, who gathered in church to listen to the readings, to meditate on them and to transform them into an effective Christian life.

---

[7] First Edition published in 1841. Refer also to Father Youhanna Tabit, *Ancient Maronite Reesh Qurian* (1242), Kaslik, 1988.

As we consulted the oldest *Reesh Qurian* that is in our possession, which is Syriac by tradition and Maronite by practice, dating back to 1242,[8] we found that the annual commemoration of the feast of the Virgin Mary is mentioned three times: (a) in the "Liturgy of the Annunciation of Mary, Mother of God"; (b) in the "Liturgy of the Visitation of Mary to Elizabeth"; and (c) in the "Liturgy of the Praises of the Mother of God, which is celebrated the day after Christmas." Besides these, there was no mention of other Marian feasts. Looking at the readings of these feasts we find a collection from the Old and the New Testaments without details or commentary at the disposal of the Lectors, with the exception of the Gospel, and they are as follows:

- In the "Liturgy of the Annunciation of Mary, Mother of God" there are ten readings, eight from the Old Testament and two from the New Testament.

- In the "Liturgy of the Visitation of Mary to Elizabeth" there are four readings, two from the Old Testament and two from the New Testament.

- In the "Liturgy of the Praises of the Mother of God" there are fifteen readings, thirteen from the Old Testament and two from the New Testament.

The rest of the collection of *Reesh Qurian* contains Gospel readings only mentioned in the Gospel Book. This Gospel book is organized according to the feasts of the year. It is a very old Book in manuscript form with several copies in Syriac, spread over reputable libraries in Lebanon and abroad.

The most important of these manuscripts is the one known by the "Gospel of Rabbula" used by the Maronites for several centuries. The table of content of this gospel cites the selected readings for the twelfth or the thirteenth century. It is almost contemporary to *Reesh Qurian* and completes the selected collection of the Gospel readings.

---

[8] Ibid.

1. The Gospel of Rabbula

In this Gospel we find the following readings for the feast of the Virgin Mary:

- The Annunciation of the Mother of God, in Luke 1:26-37

- The Visitation is also in Luke 1:39-56

- The Praises of "The Mother of God," celebrated the day after Christmas, consisting of three Gospel readings, the Evening prayer, the Morning prayers and the Divine Liturgy. They are presented respectively: The first Gospel has the sign of Jonah, in Matthew 16:1-4. The second Gospel provides the carpenter, Son of Mary, in Mark 6:1-6. The third Gospel reads: blessed is the womb that bore you..., in Luke 11:27-32

- "The Mother of God," the Gospel is in Luke 11:33-36

- "The Mother of God" and the Entrance into Lent, the Gospel of the wedding feast at Cana of Galilee is in John 2:1-11.

Going back to these texts we find either a display of the "Maronite Marian theology" or a detailed description of the personality of the Virgin Mary from the Maronite "Scriptural" point of view.

2. *Reesh Qurian*, 1242

For the various liturgical and paraliturgical services of Marian feasts like the Annunciation, the Visitation and the Praises of the Mother of God, a reading list was chosen as follows:

A. Liturgical Services of the Annunciation to Mary

1 Gn 18:1-15, The appearance of the Lord in the Terebinth of Mamre. The announcement that Sarah is going to have a son.
2 Jb 34:1-14, "Wisdom is when man listens to the command of God."

3 Jgs 13:2-7, The appearance of the Angel to the wife of Manoah. "You will bear a son..."
4 1 Kgs 8:3-11, The Ark of the Covenant of Yahweh or the Lord's glory had filled the temple of the Lord.
5 Prv 30:1-9, The Son of the Most High... "What is his name, what is his Son's name?"
6 Ez 44;1-3, The closed outer gate of the Sanctuary through which the Lord entered. This is a reference to the virginity of Mary.
7 Dn 13:1, 12, 60, 63, The praises of God that saved Susanna.
8 Is 7:10-17, The "virgin shall be with child, and bear a son, and shall name him Emmanuel."
9 1 Jn 3:2-9, Christ, the Son of God.
10 Heb 11:2-19, 'Through faith we perceive that the worlds were created by the word of God..."

B. Liturgical Services of the Visitation of Mary

1 Gn 25:19-23, The prayer of Isaac to the Lord on behalf of his sterile wife and the Lord's hearing of Isaac's prayer.
2 Is 35:3-10, "Then will the eyes of the blind be open, the ears of the deaf be cleared..."
3 1 Pt 1:5-13, Through faith "there is a cause for rejoicing here..."
4 Heb 6:9-20, 7:1-2, God fulfills his promises, Melchizedek is a symbol of Christ, "Son of God."

C. Liturgical Services of the Praises of the Mother of God

1 Ex 3:1-10, The Bush of Moses. God is in the burning Bush, which is not consumed.
2 Nm 17:1-9, Aaron's staff sprouts and flourishes...
3 Dt 10:1-5, The Ark of the Covenant, which contains the commandments of God.
4 Jb 26:1-14, "Through His powerful hand He saves...," God's effective power.
5 Jos 17:3-4, The inheritance of God is granted to daughters, not only to sons.
6 Jgs 6:36-40, Dew comes on the fleece of Gideon, while all the ground is dry.

7   I Sm 2:1-10, Hannah's hymn resembles Mary's Canticle.

8   Zec 4:8-14, The lighted "Lampstand" in the house of the Lord.

9   Prv. 30:18-28, The Virgin Mary does not know man. The Virgin Mary and the Church.

10   Bar 3:24-38; 4:1, "She has appeared on earth, and moved among men." This is a comparison of the Virgin Mary and the Church.

11   Ez 44:1-8, The closed outer gate of the Sanctuary through which the Lord entered. The Virgin Mary and the Church.

12   Dn 5:8-11, Queen Esther is the symbol of the Virgin Mary.

13   Is 19:18-25, "The altar of the Lord inside the land of Egypt."

14   Acts 7:30-39, Moses, as "an angel appeared to him in the flame of a burning thornbush...," he prophesied that the Lord who led His people out of Egypt, will raise up for them a prophet like him.

15   Rom 9:6, 16, 33, Fulfillment of the promise through the Son. This is a comparison between the son of Sarah and the Son of Mary.

What can we conclude from these readings?

Here we have numerous and very rich conclusions. Going back to each text and explaining it in light of what has been achieved, we may conclude the following:

1. The interpretation of the Old Testament is practically implied according to what has been achieved in the New Testament. The feast of the Annunciation, the Visitation or any memorial of the Virgin Mary, is the starting point from the Scriptural event. In light of this event, the texts of the Old Testament are understood and, at the same time, they explain the texts of the New Testament, which parallels this chain of Scriptural events.

2. The Virgin Mary appears not as a single person who lives a solitary life of a hermit as if she is trying to save only "her own soul," but she always appears connected with the broader journey of salvation, starting with the Book of Genesis and leading up to the Books of the New Testament. God has a saving strategy and that is the "divine plan for the salvation of humanity." Mary was to enter into this plan to accomplish with Christ, her Son, what the Lord God had promised.

3. In the Old Testament, Mary is seen as the Ark containing the "commandments of Moses," as the "dwelling place of God" and therefore, as the "temple of God." In the New Testament she is the dwelling place of the Lord God who is Christ. She is the "Church of God." She is the icon of the Church in which the Lord dwells. Not only is she the church which is made of stone, but the Church made of people—the Mystical Body of Christ.

Some of the readings used for the Praises of the Virgin Mary are the same in the Sundays of the Consecration and the Renewal of the Church (Prv 30:18-28; Bar 3:24-38, 4:1; and Ez 44:1-8).

4. Mary, Mother of the Savior, cannot be separated from the women of the Old Testament, who were a symbol for her, such as Eve, Sarah, Rebecca, the prophetess Hannah and Queen Esther.

5. Within this complete salvific plan, the Virgin Mary is likened to the fleece of Gideon. She is a Virgin who conceives and remains a virgin, just as the Holy Books have recorded and as the Prophets have foretold.

6. The Book of Revelation is not mentioned among this selection of readings and no explanation is found for Rev 12:1 "A great sign appeared in the sky, a woman clothed with the sun, with the moon under her feet..." These readings do not mention the Virgin Mary being with Jesus, neither in the proclamation of the Kingdom nor by the Cross. However, Mary is mentioned being with Jesus at the wedding of Cana of Galilee which, in fact, is the Gospel of the Entrance into Lent Sunday, just as it was noted in the table of content of the Rabbula Gospel.

7. Apparently, all the feasts of the Virgin Mary are placed in the framework of Christmas, such as the Annunciation, the Visitation and the Praises of the Mother of God. Therefore, the veneration of the Virgin Mary was connected with her being the Mother of God and through whom the promise of salvation was fulfilled. This does not nullify her role of interceding to God on our behalf. This role will be clarified when we return to the liturgical prayers and hymns that were constantly on the lips of our ancestors, which are actually the language of the Church. The same references may be found in some readings for both the Church and the feast of the Virgin Mary. These references signal to the "intercession of the Virgin Mary" for being the "dwelling place of God" just as the Church is His dwelling place.

CHAPTER III

Mary in the First Five
Christian Centuries

Having taken a journey in search of the image of the Virgin Mary through the Sacred Scriptures, it is necessary to take a brief look and see what the first five Christian centuries taught us about the Mother of God. During these centuries, especially the fourth and fifth, controversies escalated around the person of Jesus and the person of Mary. Wherever sin multiplies, there grace outpours. The teachings of the ecumenical councils and the writings of the Church Fathers have progressively intensified about this particular topic.

As we return to these distant centuries, we experience a constant witness of faith that the Church veneration of the Virgin Mary did not happen by chance nor is it rather recent. Instead, this veneration is well rooted in the early Christian doctrine, because it is closely connected to the adoration of Christ, the Son of God and her Son.

Maronite history has had great benefits in returning to these roots, because the Maronite movement grew around the Monastery of Saint Maron, right after the Council of Chalcedon. Thus, a closer look at the echoes of the teachings of the Church Fathers and the ecumenical councils provides us with the following historical stations: (1) Justin and Irenaeus in the second century; (2) The Council of Nicaea in 325; (3) The Council of Ephesus in 431; (4) Some of the fifth century Church Fathers, such as Cyril of Alexandria and Rabbula of Edessa; and (5) The Council of Chalcedon in 451.

The next chapter is specifically dedicated to the Virgin Mary in the writings of Saint Ephrem (303-373).

1. Justin and Irenaeus, the Second Century:

A. Justin around 150 A.D. stresses two points:

- Christ was born from a virgin. This claim is of a great importance not only to show respect to the virginity of Mary but to emphasize the comparison made between her and the virgin Eve.
- Just as corruption began with the disobedience of a virgin, it concluded with the obedience and the faith of the Virgin Mary. Thus, the Virgin Mary, the new Eve, becomes the one who gave life to humanity once again. The text is as follows:

Mary and Eve:

"We learned in these later times that He became man through the Virgin. Disobedience ceased in the way it started, going through the Serpent. Eve was a virgin without deceit, but as she conceived the word of the Serpent, she bore disobedience and death. Whereas, the Virgin Mary conceived through faith and joy, when the Angel Gabriel announced to her that the Spirit of the Lord will descend upon her and the power of God will overshadow her, therefore, her first-born is Holy and will be called Son of the Most High, she answered: "let it be done to me as you say." Thus, the One who was born from her, as we have indicated, is the One of whom many books have spoken, and through whom God will destroy the Serpent, its angels and all those who bear its likeness."

(Dialogue with Tripho, 100)

B. Saint Irenaeus around 185 A.D.

As for Saint Irenaeus, he starts from Justin's point to emphasize its theological meaning and to explain this comparison between the first virgin, the disobedient Eve, and the second virgin, the obedient Mary. He further compares between death through the first and redemption through the second.

Mary and Eve:

"We find that the Virgin Mary is obedient saying: 'Here I am Lord, your servant, let it be done to me as you say.' Eve disobeyed when she was a virgin. If Eve the virgin, was the spouse of Adam, disobeyed and was the cause of death for herself and for the entire human race; the Virgin Mary, the spouse of a man to whom she was betrothed, became through her obedience, for herself and for the entire human race, the cause of salvation.

The Lord descended to Sheol to bring back to himself the Patriarchs in order to give them new life in God. He became the First among the living and Adam became the First among the dead. For this very reason, Saint Luke starts the genealogy from Christ to Adam, to indicate that it is not the Church Fathers who gave life to Jesus, but instead, it is Jesus who renewed them through the announcement of life.

The knot that Eve tied through her disobedience, Mary untied through her obedience. Whatever Eve tied through her unbelief, Mary untied through her belief. If the first (Eve) disobeyed God, the second (Mary) obeyed God, as the Virgin Mary was able to intercede for the virgin Eve. Just as humanity was subjected to death through a virgin, it was freed from death through a virgin and have expiated for the disobedience of a virgin through the obedience of a virgin."

(Against the Heretics 3:22-4)

2. The Council of Nicaea, 325 A.D.

The Council of Nicaea in 325 A.D. was the starting point of countless theological debates and strong arguments defending the true faith. The Arian heresy was the main issue of this council claiming that the "Word of God" is not the Son of God in nature, and does not have in himself the same nature with the Father. He is rather a son through adoption but not in nature. The Arian teaching about the Virgin Mary has emanated from this heretical premise, and therefore, Mary cannot have the title of Mother of God.

As we look at the writings of Saint Alexander of Alexandria 328 A.D., who attended the Council of Nicaea, and the writings of Saint Athanasius, who spent his life defending this council, we find that both of their teachings about Christ the "Son of God," about Mary the "Mother of Jesus, the Son of God" and thus Mary's title the "Mother of God" are clear, but without having articulated the term (Theotokos). The teachings of Ephesus have not as of yet appeared in detail, but they have appeared logically and theologically. Later, the Council of Ephesus needed only to clarify the divinity of Christ.

The second ecumenical council which took place in Constantinople in 381 A.D. accepted the Nicaean doctrine of faith and completed it to be more global, as addressed by the Fathers to the Universal Church, which is known today as the Creed: "We believe in one God..." in it we read "... For us men and for our salvation, he came down from Heaven: by the power of the Holy Spirit he was born of the Virgin Mary and became man..."

This is the first doctrine of the faith, as far as we know, wherein it mentions the "Virgin" Mary. From Nicaea developed the teachings and the explanations of the Church Fathers. Suffice it to mention that, the Syriac poet, Saint Ephrem, was called the "Marian Poet," because he praised the Mother of Jesus, the Blessed Mary in the majority of his hymns, and spread the teachings of Nicaea about the divinity of Jesus.

The next chapter is dedicated in its entirety to the writings of Saint Ephrem regarding the Virgin Mary because of his importance in the Maronite Liturgy and his influence over it.

3. The Council of Ephesus, 431 A.D.

Theological currents emerged in the fourth and fifth centuries about the divinity and the humanity of the Lord Jesus. Two conflicting schools surfaced: the first in Antioch emphasizing the difference between the two natures; the second in Alexandria stressing the oneness between the two natures. The issue is difficult to decipher even for theologians and experts, let alone the average person.

Everyone believes in the doctrine which teaches that Christ is God and Man. Debates were heightened as to how and when the divinity and the humanity were united in Christ; and whether they appeared in His one person or in the nature. These detailed issues entered into the various disputing groups of the Church and confused the people.

When Nestorius, who is of the school of Antioch, became the bishop of Constantinople in 428, some of his followers began preaching in the churches that the second person of the Holy Trinity was united in Christ, i.e., the man whom Mary conceived. Therefore, Mary is the mother of Christ the man (Christotokos), she is not entitled to be called (Theotokos) "Mother of God". This infers that there are two persons in Christ, one whose mother is Mary, the other whose mother is not Mary. This confused the followers of Nestorius because they did not differentiate between the one person of Christ and his two natures. Unity in Christ became in their view between Christ—God a (person) and Christ—man, another (person). As a result, in their erroneous view, Mary is only the "Mother of Jesus" and not the "Mother of God," who is also a divine person.

The opposing party headed by Cyril, the bishop of Alexandria, who invited all the bishops of the world to attend the ecumenical council that was held in Ephesus in 431 to defend the truth. Pope Celestine appointed two bishop delegates to attend the council's session and to proclaim the Church Doctrine through a letter addressed to the general assembly.

After urging Nestorius to refrain from his erroneous thoughts, the Council proclaimed that the divinity and the humanity of Christ are one entity in one God who is Christ the Son; and that He who was born from the Blessed Virgin Mary is not only Christ the Man, but also Christ the Son. The Fathers thus proclaim that the Virgin Mary truly deserves to be called (Theotokos) the "**Mother of God**." Cyril then read twelve counts of excommunication the first of which expresses this truth by saying: "Everyone who does not believe that Emmanuel is truly God and that Mary is the Mother of God because she bore him, according to the flesh, the 'Incarnate Word of God,' let him be anathema." This means that the Mystery of Incarnation cannot be understood unless the Virgin Mary is called the "Mother of God" because she is the mother of the one person, the Incarnate Son of God, the true God and the true Man. Thus, she is the true mother to this one person. The title Theotokos, "Mother of God" proved the true meaning of the Mystery of Incarnation. The Dogma that was proclaimed in Ephesus is very important because it clearly confirms the Incarnation of God who truly and completely took our human nature, not just the complete incarnation of the divine nature but also the incarnation of the second divine person. Therefore, Mary is the "dwelling place of God," she is "full of grace" and the "Mother of my Lord." This is the great mystery that the Church Fathers have explained such as Ephrem, long before Ephesus, then later Cyril, Rabbula and many others in Ephesus.

The following testimonies are those of Cyril and Rabbula:

4. Cyril of Alexandria and Rabbula of Edessa:

A. Cyril wrote to his Eparchy in Alexandria describing the joyful demonstration in the city saying:

"No doubt that your piety prompts me to inform you in detail about the events but the postman is rushing me so I shall be brief. Let it be known that on June 22 the holy council convened in Ephesus, in the great Cathedral consecrated to Mary, the Mother of God. After one full day, we concluded the trial against the non-believer Nestorius, who did not have the courage to appear at the council. The number of attendees exceeded two hundred bishops; so we excommunicated him and removed him from his position. The entire population of the city gathered around the church since the early hours of the day waiting for the decision of the holy council. When they learned about the excommunication of the poor man, they all started shouting, in one voice, praising the council and giving thanks to God for defeating the enemy of the Faith. As we left in the evening, all the people accompanied us home carrying lighted lamps. A joyful demonstration overcrowded the entire city which was brightly lighted by all sorts of festive lights to the point where even some women processed in front of us carrying censors with perfumed burning incense. This is how the Lord has shown his infinite power to those who wanted to rob Him of His glory."

(Saint Cyril of Alexandria 440)

B. In 435 A.D. Saint Rabbula of Edessa addressed one of the churches in Constantinople about the motherhood of Mary. According to its text in Syriac we read the following:

Mary, Mother of God:

"The issue about which you asked us for an answer is this: Is the Virgin Mary truly the Mother of God, or is she just called as such? Is she truly deserving of this title?

Through our unwavering hope which is our life, and through our perfect confidence which is our pride, we loudly proclaim that Mary is rightfully the Mother of God, who was truly found on earth the Mother of God the Word through his own will, because according to his nature, he has no mother in heaven. Thus the Apostle proclaimed that God sent His Son to be born of a woman. If anyone dare profess that she gave birth to God the Word in his divine nature, not only would he have claimed a wrongful statement, but rather he would have committed a blasphemy. We call her the Blessed Virgin Mary, Mother of God not because we believe she gave birth to the divine nature of Christ, but because from her was born God, the Incarnate Word. The virgin will give birth to a son and will call him Emmanuel, which translates God is with us. Our Lord did not take His original divine nature from the Virgin Mary, because He is the Word who, in the beginning, was with God as John had testified. But because of His mercy, He appeared from Mary as Christ, in his human nature. He is the true God, ranking above every creature...

This is our faith: He who was with God from the beginning, God the Word, was born in his divine nature from the Father, and in due time, he was born according to the flesh from the Virgin Mary for our salvation..."

5. The Council of Chalcedon, 451 A.D.

All the teachings that were promulgated at the Council of Ephesus were fully adopted by the Council of Chalcedon and further clarified the unity of both the divine and the human natures in the person of Christ... Thence, Eastern Christianity was divided into two parties: One sided with the Council of Chalcedon, i.e., Pope Leo (440-461) and the Byzantine Emperor; the other opposed the council and the Emperor.

The Maronites were not considered simple adherents to the Council of Chalcedon, but they were accused of being planted in the East to defend it. They were staunch supporters to its teachings to the point where common slogans described them as follows: "The Maronites are the grapevine which was planted by Pope Leo," and "The Maronites are the King's Men" (the king here is the Byzantine Emperor).

Many Maronites sacrificed their lives for the sake of this council; the most notable are the 350 martyrs who were massacred in 516 at the hands of the non-Chalcedonians. The teachings of this council are summarized in the letter that Pope Leo addressed to the Fathers who convened in Chalcedon in 451. The Pope writes:

> "We believe in God the Father maker of all things, in His only Son, our Lord Jesus Christ who was born of the Virgin Mary, by the power of the Holy Spirit. Through these three, the ammunitions of the heretics and their powers were destroyed, because when a person believes that God the Father is the all powerful one, then, that person is given the proof that the Son existed with the Father from the beginning, and does not differ from Him in anything. He was begotten while he is God from God, all powerful from Him who is all powerful. The Son does not differ from the Father in glory, nor is he separated from the Father in essence. But he is the only Son, the eternal Son from the eternal Father, born from the Holy Spirit and the Virgin Mary. This birth, in due time, did neither take away, nor add anything to that eternal divine birth..."

> "Therefore, the same person who is the image of God, became man in the image of the servant, because the two natures were

preserved in essence without any change. Just as the image of God did not negate or eliminate the image of the servant, in like manner, the image of the servant did not distort the image of God..."

"The amazing birth of our Lord Jesus through the womb of Mary, does not mean that his nature differs from ours, because he is a true God and a true man. There is neither imagining nor hallucination in this unity when the lowliness of humanity meets the loftiness of divinity..."

When the letter of Pope Leo was read to the Fathers of the Council they all shouted: "This is the faith of the Fathers, this is the faith of the Apostles. Peter is speaking through the mouth of Leo."

Shortly hereafter, the ecumenical council defined the doctrine of the faith as follows:

"As we follow in the footsteps of the venerable Fathers, we teach in one solid opinion and must confess that the Son, our Lord Jesus Christ, is the same one himself being completely divine and completely human, true God and true man, equal in essence to the Father and equal to us in humanity. He is like us in everything except sin, begotten of the Father according to his divinity before all ages, but in due time, for us men and for our salvation, he was born of the Virgin Mary, Mother of God, according to the flesh. This one person is himself Jesus Christ, the only Son who must be confessed as being united in two natures without mixture, transformation, division or separation."

The Council of Chalcedon has a special echo in the history of the Maronites. They are the children and the product of this Council, because without it they would not have been any different from all the other Syriac Antiochene. Therefore, their adherence to the letter of Pope Leo and to the teachings of Chalcedon did accompany them on their spiritual journey which was reflected in their liturgical prayers and in their attachment to the Virgin Mary, the Mother of Jesus, God—man, the one person in two natures, and consequently, the true 'Mother of God.'" This is what will be clearly revealed in our rituals and liturgical services.

CHAPTER IV

Mary in the Writings of Saint Ephrem

Saint Ephrem was born in Nisibis in 303 and died in Edessa in 373. He wrote in Syriac both poetry and prose. Without any doubt, he is one of the greatest Syriac Fathers. He is known as the Doctor of the Universal Church and the harp of the Holy Spirit. The Church has never known anyone like Saint Ephrem who praised the Virgin Mary "before the Council of Ephesus." Just like the other Syriac Churches, our Maronite Church considers him not only an "instructor and interpreter" but rather "its own Teacher." He is the unifying figure among all the Syriac Churches. His teachings about the Virgin Mary are detailed in this chapter.

Saint Ephrem did not dedicate one particular volume of his writings to explain his theological thoughts about the Virgin Mary. Scholars familiar with his writings would not recommend one specific book on this topic. Many articles are published in different languages about the Virgin Mary by Ephrem, the most complete and recent of which is the work of Father Ortiz De Urbina. Most of the references herewith draw on his work.[9]

It is a well-known fact that Saint Ephrem dedicated his theological revelation to the Virgin Mary in many of his hymns and scriptural commentaries. This also served as a continuation of his theological revelation about Jesus, because during his times, he had to defend

---

[9] Refer to this Article for all the following references.
  I. Ortiz De Urbina, *La Vergine Maria nella teologia di S. Ephrem, Symposium Syriacum 1972*. Orientala Christiana Analecta, 197, (pp. 5-104).

against the heresies of Marcion and Arius, which were widely spread in the Church:

1. The Marcion heresy claimed that Christ is not truly human like all people but "he was compared to a man," he appeared like a man, this is why, in reality Mary is not the Mother of Jesus, the Savior, who has no mother in the flesh.

2. The Arian heresy claimed that Christ is not the Son of God in nature but has become the Son of God through adoption. In fact, Jesus is human like all other creatures. He appeared as a man like all humans and God adopted him later. Therefore, the Virgin Mary is not the "Mother of the Divine Word" but the mother of a great man...

In opposition of these two heresies, and according to the true teachings of the Church which excommunicated Marcion then Arius in the Council of Nicaea in 325, Saint Ephrem taught through hymns and explained the Sacred Scriptures preaching that Jesus is the true Son of God, the Incarnate Word of God, who created both heaven and earth and he dwelt in the womb of the Virgin Mary who became the "Mother of her Son, his sister and his daughter..."

The writings of Saint Ephrem about the Virgin Mary, by far surpass the writings of all the Fathers who wrote in other languages or who belonged to other Churches in the East or in the West. His most famous writings about the Virgin Mary are as follows:

- The Commentary on the Diatessaron, more than half of which is in Syriac, is preserved in its entirety in Armenian.
- The Hymns on the Nativity (2, 4, 6, 8, 9, 11, 12)
- The Hymns of Nisibis, especially: (4, 27, 35, 37)
- The Hymns on the Virginity, especially: (96, 13, 25, 38)
- The Hymns on the "Church," especially: (35, 37, 46, 49)
- The Hymns on the "Doctrine of the Faith," especially: (4, 10, 24, 28, 51, 60, 73, 74)
- Various Hymns such as the Paradise: 4, the Unleavened Bread: 4, 16, the Crucifixion: 3, and the Resurrection: 1, 4.

Based on these hymns and commentaries, it is evident that Ephrem did not publish doctrinal or theological writings modeled after any particular scholastic method, but he composed poetry and wrote commentaries, following the sequential explanation of the Sacred Scriptures. He then studied the texts and the symbols; he provided commentaries and explanations in unison with the Church doctrine and unveiled the complete mystery of the divine plan.

The Marian revelation of Ephrem can be classified in three major concepts:

1.   Mary is the Mother of the Lord Jesus.
2.   Mary is the Ever-Virgin.
3.   Mary is the New Eve.

There are many other branching thoughts about the characteristics of the Virgin Mary which were revealed by the poetry of Ephrem. Only a few of them are mentioned in detail about these basic thoughts.

1. Mary is the Mother of the Lord Jesus

A. Mary is truly a Mother. Ephrem knew that Edessa, the territory of Bardesanes, was not foreign to the agnostic thoughts which claimed that Jesus is a "man-like" figure who did not come to the world in an earthly body but in a "heavenly" body. Therefore, in their view, Jesus was not born of the Virgin Mary, but he came to the world through her without her giving him anything.

Ephrem clearly explains in his Hymns on the Faith that Jesus is truly the Son of God and the Son of Mary and therefore, "He became a brother to mankind." Commenting on Luke 11:27; "Blessed is the womb that conceived you and the breasts that nursed you..." he answers Marcion and details how Jesus is in reality a brother to every person and therefore, proved that Mary gave birth according to the flesh just like all women. In his commentary, he goes back to the Sacred Scriptures where he finds that Jesus is the "Son of David" and that Joseph and Mary were from the lineage of David, Luke 2:4; that "The Lord God will give him the throne of David his father," Luke 1:32; and that Jesus, the "Son of Mary" is also the son of David.

Therefore, she is truly his mother who made him the heir of the throne of his father David.

To further clarify the true motherhood of Mary, Ephrem says: God is in need of a true body and must be truly human in order to save mankind. He had acquired this humanity through the womb of the Virgin Mary. In this way, he became a humble servant to save mankind: "The womb of your Mother had changed the theories, because the Creator of all entered it wealthy and came out of it poor, he entered it as a lofty person and came out of it as a lowly person..."

Ephrem mentions in detail that the Virgin conceived Jesus on the tenth of April and she gave birth in January, thirteen days before the brightest day of the Sun (Hymns on the Nativity).

As far as being the Mother of Jesus, Ephrem wrote purely angelic hymns about relations between mother and child, and composed sweet poems on behalf of a mother as she whispers to her nursing child as to how she would softly talk to the sleeping baby in his crib or on her arms; how she would rock him singing the hymns of a mother who is filled with devotion; "How can I nourish you with milk and you are the source! How can I feed the one who feeds all creation! How can I get close to your cheeks, you who are clothed in glory?" (Hymns on the Nativity: 14 and 15).

In his words about the sayings of Jesus at the Cross: "Behold your mother... Behold your son," Ephrem brings about a psychological side of Mary in theological term with the most beautiful form of poetry: "Blessed are you O woman, because your Lord and your Son has given you, to whom he has made according to his image. You caressed Jesus as a child and Jesus caressed John when he leaned against His chest... You nursed Jesus from your chest a visible drink and Jesus nursed John from His side an invisible drink. With such comfort Jesus leaned his head on your chest...and with such comfort John leaned his head on Jesus' chest... He left you but he did not forsake you, because he came back with his disciple to live with you... Mary saw Jesus in his disciple and, with love and respect, the disciple honored the Temple in which she lived..."

(Hymns on the Virginity: 25)

B.   Mary is the Mother of God. Ephrem died about one half of a century before the Council of Ephesus. The title "The Mother of God" had not yet found its way to the Church and that is why it appeared somewhat different on the tongue of Ephrem. But his teachings about the Virgin Mary being the Mother of God are quite clear; in many of his writings, they are very decisive on this issue.

In his *Diatessaron*[10], Ephrem proves that the Incarnate Word who was in the bosom of the Father is the same who became the Son of the Virgin: "Elizabeth, the daughter of Aaron gave birth to the voice of the wilderness, but the daughter of King David gave birth to the wisdom of the heavenly king. The wife of the priest gave birth to the angel of the Lord, whereas the daughter of David gave birth to God, the powerful Lord of the earth."

In the *Hymns on the Nativity*, Ephrem writes in great length about the motherhood of the Virgin Mary to the Divine Word: "She carried the silent child in whom all tongues were hidden." "He is the Most High, yet He fed on the milk of Mary, whereas all creation feed on his abundant riches."

In some of these *Hymns on the Nativity*, especially in the eighth and the ninth, there are expressions that come close to the title of the "Mother of God" without actually pronouncing it wherein he says: "What mother can chant to her son as did Mary? What woman would dare call her son the Son of the Creator; who is she who called her son the Son of the Most High... What mother can address her son as if she is praying to him: 'you are the hope of your mother just like God'?"

---

[10] Diatessaron is a Greek term which means "the unified version from the four Gospels." Tatian published in Greek this "unified Gospel" in the second century. It was translated into Syriac and during the time of Saint Ephrem it was read in churches. Saint Ephrem wrote a Commentary on it, but only one half of it is left in Syriac. This Commentary was translated into Armenian since the fifth century and is preserved in its entirety.

In conclusion, one can say that Ephrem believed, without any doubt, that the son of Mary is the Lord himself in the full divine sense of the word! He is the Most High, the Creator and the Son of God. Ephrem did infer this doctrine from his genuine Commentary on the Diatessaron and from delving into the Sacred Scriptures. He taught this doctrine within the Syriac Antiochene framework before the Council of Ephesus came to be, outside the renowned School of Antioch that was later dominated by Theodorus and Theodoret...

2. Mary is the Ever-Virgin

The Antiochene and Syriac authors have shown this characteristic of Mary since their early writings; that is what Ignatius wrote, and what the *Odes of Solomon* taught, in the beginning of the second century. But Ephrem further praised this virginity at the Conception, at the Birth and after the Birth.

As for the virginity in the Conception of Jesus, he explained what was written in the Gospel, that He who is from her is from the Holy Spirit. There are numerous texts about this subject: "She conceived without a man, just as in the beginning Eve was taken from Adam without a seed." Jesus dwelt in the womb of Mary after the Angel greeted her and delivered to her the heavenly message. That is why Ephrem, along with countless Syriac Fathers after him, says that "death entered through the ears of Eve and life entered through the ears of Mary."

Through his poetic genius and deep spirituality, Ephrem writes that "Jesus comes forth four times:" the first, from the bosom of the Father; the second, from the womb of Mary; the third, from the Jordan River; and the fourth, from among the dead. Each and every exit is a birth, thus, each and every birth is a new life: "The womb of the mother and Sheol (the dwelling place of the dead) announce your resurrection. The womb carried you while it was sealed and Sheol received you while it was closed."

As for the virginity and the Birth of Jesus, Ephrem explained it in his Commentary on the Diatessaron and in the Hymns on the Nativity.

One of the sayings reads: "She was a virgin when in holiness she gave birth to you who are all holy." When talking about the Birth of Jesus, Ephrem spoke of a holy, pure and mysterious birth, just as was his conception. Although in some texts he spoke about the pains and sufferings that accompanied the birth, he never mentioned that Mary lost her virginity while giving birth.

Speaking about the virginity of Mary after the birth of Jesus, in his Commentary on the Diatessaron Ephrem says:

> "Some people claim that Mary became the wife of Joseph after the birth of the Savior. How can this be that she, who became the dwelling place of the Holy Spirit, i.e., the dwelling place of God, she who was overshadowed by the divine power of the Most High, could possibly become the spouse of a mortal man giving birth and undergoing pains and sufferings according to the first curse? Just as she conceived in purity, she remained in purity. Just as the miracle of the jars of water in Cana of Galilee was never repeated, so the Virgin Mary, who conceived and gave birth to Emmanuel, never conceived ever after."

When "these same people" claim that Jesus had brothers, Ephrem notes in his Commentary on the Diatessaron:

> "Just because some were called the brothers of the Lord, it was assumed that they are Mary's children. Mary gave birth to her first-born Son and her virginity remained intact. If Jesus had brothers, our Lord would never have entrusted his Mother to John! Because it is he who said honor you father and mother, so how and why would he put a barrier between the mother and her children by giving her to John?"

Arianism was widely spread during the time of Ephrem, there is no need to be reminded that he taught against it. In fact, he was still young when the Church condemned Arianism. That is why Ephrem emphasized the Divinity of Jesus and, consequently, the holiness of the conception and the birth. He did not teach through vague poetry, but in crystal clear explanation of the Gospel, in the light of the teachings of the Sacred Scriptures and in fulfilling the symbols and the sayings of the prophets.

3. Mary is the New Eve

A. Mary and Eve: One of the Marian symbols, which caught Ephrem's attention and prompted him to discuss it in detail, is the face of Mary as the "New Eve." This comparison was used by Justin in the middle of the second century and by Irenaeus toward the end of the same century. However, in Ephrem's writings we find numerous texts and complete explanations to this comparison between Christ and Adam and between Mary and Eve.

The face of Mary as the new Eve will put her in the heart of the divine providence. God from the very beginning established a plan to save humanity and as soon as he created Adam he planned his salvation. Thus, Mary was to Christ just as Eve was to Adam:

> "Just as in the beginning Eve was born from Adam without blemish, such was Mary, the spouse of Joseph. Eve gave birth to a killer, whereas Mary gave birth to the Giver of Life. Eve gave birth to the one who shed the blood of his brother, whereas Mary gave birth to the One who shed his own blood for his brethren. Eve gave birth to the one who fled from the curse of the earth, whereas Mary gave birth to the One who bore the curse and nailed it by his cross."

In many of his Hymns, Ephrem makes a comparison between Mary the Blessed and Eve the "cursed" thus Elizabeth proclaimed: "Blessed are you among women, this infers that the first mother was cursed."

When Mary would chant to her baby a lullaby, she would say: "I will enter into his paradise, the paradise of life, and wherein Eve failed, I will glorify him."

When Christ descended into Sheol, Eve rejoiced. Because the Son of her daughter came down as medicine for life to raise the mother of his Mother! "The blessed Son crushed the head of the serpent who deceived Eve." "In paradise, Eve wore the leaves of embarrassment, whereas your Mother wore the robe of glory which envelops all." In his Hymns on the Church, Ephrem teaches how the Virgin Mary is the one who gave life which the world lost through Eve:

> "It is quite clear that Mary is the land of the Sun, i.e., the land from which the sun shines, which has enlightened the world and its inhabitants, this world which was darkened because of Eve, the root of all evils. Eve and Mary are likened to the two eyes of the one face: the one eye is blind and darkened, while the other is wide open and has enlightened everything. Look at the world in which two eyes were placed: Eve, the left eye, is the eye of darkness; Mary, the right eye, is the eye of brightness. Because of the darkened eye, the entire world became dark where people worship idols instead of God and proclaimed lies as the truth. When the world was enlightened, through the brightened eye and the Heavenly Light that dwelt in it, the world found unity again and discovered that 'what it had known all along was the loss of life.' "

In his comparison between the words of the serpent to Eve in paradise and the words of the Angel to Mary during the Annunciation, Ephrem derides the foolishness of Eve for believing the serpent without any hesitation or attentiveness, whereas the wise Mary, was posing questions to the Angel:

> "Let us, with admiration, meditate on Mary who asked the Archangel without fear. Eve never attempted to ask the deceiving serpent, whereas the young maiden stood in the presence of Gabriel and asked him, because she had not known yet who he was. Mary asked the Angel for a clarification to this truth, whereas Eve accepted all the liar's deceptions. The foolish mother is the cause of all our tribulations, whereas the prudent sister is the treasure of all our joy."

In his "Hymn about Our Lord," Ephrem describes the position of Eve and that of Mary about life and death when Christ entered the abode of the dead:

> "Eve the mother of all the living came forth... Eve who was the mother of every living human became the source of death to every one. Mary appeared as the new shoot of Eve who represented the old life. When death made its way, between the dead fruits, through its normal deception, there appeared the New Life which issued through Mary and devoured death."

All these texts confirmed the role of Mary in salvation. She was very closely connected with Christ, just as Eve was connected with Adam. We cannot consider the Virgin Mary a saint like all the other saints in the Church. She is rather a blessed shoot who gave life instead of the cursed one who brought death.

This old comparison between Eve and Mary took to a new horizon with Ephrem who adorned it and generously gave it shining and glowing colors. These deep theological thoughts about Mary have a great echo in the relation of Mary and the Church and consequently in the Eucharist, the Bread of life. All these beautiful comparisons between the lighted eye and the darkened eye take us to the heart of the Gospel which makes of Eve, the image of the sinful humanity, who is far from God and makes of Mary, the image of the obedient disciple of Christ, who becomes a witness to the Faith.

B. The Pure Mary: As far as we know, among Church Fathers of both Eastern and Western Traditions, Ephrem alone spoke with complete clarity about the purity of the Virgin Mary who was perfected in a special favor from God. In his view, Mary's purity is intertwined with her motherhood to the Incarnate Word and with her role in overcoming sin.

This teaching of Ephrem became clear especially in the Hymns of Nisibis. In Hymn 27, the Church of Edessa calls the Lord Jesus saying:

> "If I am ugly do not divorce me. Love me, I who am ugly, and teach as such that every man must love his wife, even if she is ugly. You and your Mother alone are beautiful in everything among all creatures, because

there is no ugliness about you, O Lord, and there is no blemish in your Mother."

The idea of Saint Ephrem is explained as follows: The Edessa Church community has some ugliness, but it also has dignified faithful. However, the case of Jesus and his Mother is different from the common people in purity and chastity, as if he is saying: all people have the "ugliness of sin," but "there is no such ugliness" in Jesus and his Mother.

Does this mean that Ephrem was talking about Original sin and about the Virgin Mary, the "Immaculate Conception," just as Pope Pius IX proclaimed in the year 1854?

We must not shed new light upon old history of the Church. But one can conclude from the letter of Pope Pius IX about the Immaculate Conception the same view that Ephrem stressed, i.e., that the Virgin Mary never committed any failure or sin. All the comparisons that Ephrem always gave about Mary as the "new Eve..." and about her role in the journey of salvation, confirmed to us that God freed Mary from any stain of sin. Bear in mind that the Church gradually defined the doctrine of "Original Sin."

In the view of Ephrem, this did not mean that the Virgin Mary was, like Christ, pure in nature, but she was made pure through the grace of the Spirit who sanctified her. When he speaks of the sanctity of Mary, he means that her holiness is through the grace of her Son Jesus to whom she became a disciple, was "baptized" and received the Eucharist. Baptism, in his opinion, was given the Virgin Mary so that she becomes the "daughter of the Lord," not necessarily to erase the stain of Original Sin, because the Church Doctrine at the time was not yet quite as clear about it.

Summary

Mary had a great part in the Hymns of Saint Ephrem and in his commentaries on the Sacred Scriptures. His thoughts were not just mere attractive poetic tangents, but rather deep theological meditations motivated by pure love to Jesus and his Mother. God granted Mary many favors, especially her divine motherhood, her perpetual virginity and her great role in the salvific plan and thus, her purity, her sanctity and her place in being so close to Jesus.

In conclusion, it must be clarified that Ephrem did not speak about the death of the Virgin Mary or about her Assumption in body and soul into Heaven. Like all Church Fathers of that particular period, he believed that the souls who are in paradise, "they rest in the hope of the Resurrection."

Ephrem provided basic theological thoughts about Mary in truth and reality whereby they no longer were his personal property, these hymns and teachings have penetrated the Maronite Syriac Liturgy. As we shall see, these thoughts are quite visible in our present-day hymns and prayers. In order to complete these thoughts we shall provide three poems from Saint Ephrem about the Virgin Mary: Two of them are from the collection of the "Blessed Mary" and the third is from the collection of his Hymns on the Nativity:

Three Hymns from Saint Ephrem

>   A. Who is the Virgin Mary.
>   B. The Mystery of Redemption.
>   C. The Nativity of Jesus.

A. Who is the Virgin Mary

Ephrem here emphasizes the phenomenon of the two opposites. She is a virgin and a mother. She is a young dove who is expecting an offspring for an eagle, who is ancient of days. She is pure and chaste carrying Good News and peace to humanity. She ranks high as she carries on her knees, the One whom heavens cannot hold as if she is greater than the heavens.

> O come, all you who are wise, let us meditate with amazement,
> the virgin mother, the daughter of David;
> the honorable mother who is full of wonder;
> the stream that overflowed with the spring;
> the ship of joy who carries the Good News from the Father;

she carried in her pure womb the marvelous creator of all;
through whom peace reigned in heaven and on earth.

O come, let us meditate with amazement, the pure one who is
full of wonder;
because she alone, among all creatures, gave birth without
intercourse;
the soul of the pure one was filled with amazement, every day
she praised God with joy as Virgin and Mother! Blessed is he
who dawned from her!

A young dove is expecting an offspring for an eagle, who is
ancient of days, and praising him with love songs: O richly
child, O harp whose melodies are silent like a child, command
that I sing to you on a harp whose melodies are played by the
Cherubim, command and I shall sing to you.

There is no loftier rank than yours, O my son, yet you willed to
make me your dwelling place.
Heavens cannot hold your glory, yet the Virgin carries you.
Let Ezekiel come and see you on my knees, let him kneel and
worship you, let him witness that you are the One that he saw
there.

Let Him who sits on the chariot of the Cherubim in the highest
Heaven call me blessed for the sake of the One I carry.

(Hymns about the Blessed Virgin Mary, 7)

B. The Mystery of Redemption

She is a virgin and a mother, a pure saint, an honorable and a
perfectly beautiful one. She brings joy and Good News to all nations,
from Adam until today. She is an image of the Church in all of its
various aspects:

- As a virgin: she is the joy of virgins.

- As a daughter of Adam: she cured humanity from the sting of
  the serpent.

- As a mother: she is the mother of the High Priest and of all priests.

- Through her the sayings of the Prophets were fulfilled and the saints were made holy...

    1. The Virgin Mary invited me to proclaim her mystery and I was amazed by it! O Son of God grant me your wondrous talents so that I may tune my harp and play the most beautiful songs for your Mother.

    2. In her womb there is life, not intercourse; she is amazing, she is great; in her breasts there is milk, what an extraordinary event, in her pure body, virginity and motherhood were united, what an amazing mystery! Who can speak about it?

    3. In holiness, the Virgin Mary gave birth to her Son, with her milk she nursed the One who satisfies all nations, on her knees she carried the One who carries the world, she is Virgin and Mother; what cannot she be!

    4. She is holy in body, beautiful in soul, pure in spirit, unsurpassed in understanding, complete in sensitivity, chaste, innocent, immaculate in heart, and perfect in beauty.

    5. Let all virgins rejoice in Mary, because one of them gave birth to the all powerful One who carries all creation, through whom enslaved humanity was set free.

    6. Let Adam, who was stung by the serpent, rejoice in Mary for she granted him a well disposed offspring. Through the offspring, Adam overcame Satan and was freed from the sting of the deadly serpent.

    7. Let all priests rejoice in the Blessed Virgin for she gave birth to the High Priest who became a Sacrifice and spared them from all sacrifices; for He became the sacrifice and pleased His Father.

8. Let the entire line of Prophets rejoice in Mary for through her all their revelations were fulfilled, their prophecies were completed and through her, all their sayings were confirmed.

9. Let the assembly of the Patriarchs rejoice in Mary, for as she received their blessing, she perfected them through her Son. Through her, the visionaries, the Just, and the Priest were all purified.

10. Mary gave mankind a sweet and precious fruit instead of that bitter fruit which Eve picked from the tree. Therefore, all creation enjoys the fruit of Mary.

11. The tree of life, hidden in Paradise, it was completed through Mary and from her it sprung forth while creation rested in its shade, it showered its fruits upon those who are far and near.

12. Mary knitted the robe of glory and gave it to her father who was naked between the trees, with it he was clothed, covered, and adorned in beauty; while his wife struck him, his daughter restored him and he arose victoriously.

13. Eve and the serpent set a trap in which Adam fell, Mary and the King hastened, bent down and brought him out of the hole, through the hidden mystery of Him who was transfigured, and revived mankind.

14. The Virgin's vineyard produced the grape of good wine, through it those who were distressed found peace in their misery, Adam and Eve tasted the medicine of life and their anguish vanished.

(Hymns about the Blessed Virgin Mary)

C. The Nativity of Jesus

How meaningful and beautiful is this hymn in describing the Virgin Mary. Imploring Jesus, Saint Ephrem says: "She is your mother, your sister, your bride and your maiden."

"O you who are the Teacher of his own mother, you who are the Lord of his own mother, you who are the God of his own mother... You have mystified your creation."

Mary is the mother of the One who is rocked on her knees and the One who is clothed in divinity.

1. Lord, who are most infinite, I begin my prayers speaking of you and conclude them by depending on you. I open my mouth to praise your humility, you, O Lord, fill my mouth from your treasures. I am the earth and you are the tiller, sow your word in the mouth of an incapable man. You planted yourself in the pure Virgin, you were born through virginity, you dawned from the Father and took flesh from Mary who had borne fruit without insemination.

2. Mary gave birth to the all powerful and all knowledgeable One, who is hidden in nature and clothed in Divinity. She holds him, she sings to him and hugs him. He swiftly throws himself in her lap, he stares at her with a smile like a little babe in a manger. She wraps him in swaddling clothes and she tucks him in. If he cries, she hastens to nurse him, she embraces him, and she rocks him on her knees so that he may be well entertained.

3. David, your father, chanted for you before you came, you, who are God's only Son. In his hymns he prophesied about the gold of Saba and his prophecy was truly fulfilled. The gold, the frankincense and the myrrh are placed before you. The gold is for your kingship, the frankincense is for your divinity and the myrrh is for your humanity, blessed are those who find no doubt in you...!

4. Mary is your mother, your sister, your bride and your maiden, yet she also gave you birth. She called you, she embraced you and she kissed you, then she glorified, prayed and gave thanks. She nursed you with her milk and pressed you to her chest; and while she was playing with you, smiling at your childhood, you were suckling her milk and rolling with joy.

You have mystified your mother who has held you; you have mystified your creation! Dear Son, allow your mother to take good care of you.

5. You who are the teacher of his own Mother, you who are her Lord and God; you are younger than she, yet you are much more ancient. Please be still, you have exhausted me, and your love has drained me. Who could see you and not admire you. Your beauty has blinded the onlookers and your appearance has silenced the eloquent. Behold, your hands are tied, your feet are kicking, how gentle you are in your entirety, for your mouth is full of praise to your Father...

(Hymns on the Nativity)

CHAPTER V

Mary and the History of the
Maronite Liturgy

Throughout history, between its inception in the fifth century and its present-day reality, the Maronite Liturgy has passed through several stages. Manuscripts and published resources inform us about these stages from the fifteenth century until today. However, if there exists a paucity of such references between the tenth and the fifteenth, what could one say about the five-century period situated between the fifth and the tenth?

We shall attempt to consult resources in these historical periods, incomplete as they may be, stretching from the fifth century until today. Then we shall draw whatever conclusion possible about the beginning of the Maronite Liturgy and its development throughout these periods and show how this development has affected and shaped the Marian doctrine in thoughts and devotions.

1. The Maronite Liturgy:
From Saint Maron until Saint John Maron, 400-700

This period consists of the initial stage, beginning with the glowing fame of Saint Maron the hermit, passing through the Ecumenical Councils: Ephesus in 431, Chalcedon in 451, Constantinople in 553 and in 681 along with the divisions that followed among Christians in the Antiochene Church. Following the split between the Eastern and the Western Syriac Churches which resulted from the Council of Ephesus, the Western Syriac also split among themselves between Melkites, those loyal to the Emperor at the Council of Chalcedon and the non-Chalcedonians, who adopted the theory of the one nature in Christ, later known as Jacobites. Lastly, the Chalcedonians were divided among themselves in the seventh century about whether there was one or two wills in Christ.

In spite of all these ideological divisions, the Liturgy was never divided in the beginning. There was only one common Liturgy for all the various traditions, however, particular liturgical components and different liturgical currents dominated each of them.

As for the Maronites, through Saint Maron, they were close to John Chrysostom, to Theodoret of Cyrrhus and to the Greek Antiochene heritage. It is our belief that after the Council of Chalcedon the Monastery of Saint Maron has continued this relation with Antioch, with the Roman Church and the Byzantine Emperor. Their closeness to the West does not mean that they were far from the Syriac Edessene culture and its Liturgy. Based on *Sharrar*, one of their most ancient *Anaphora* which greatly resembles the Eastern Syriac *Anaphora*, we believe that the Maronites possess a liturgical prayer strongly rooted both in the Eastern and the Western Syriac Liturgies since the fifth century.

We can safely claim that between the fifth and the seventh century, the Liturgy of the Monastery of Saint Maron drew on three basic Eastern liturgical sources: Antioch, Jerusalem and Edessa. Spiritual and historical manuscripts from that period indicate that the Maronites were well versed in Greek and Syriac. However, beginning with the seventh century, they gradually began to abandon the Greek for the Syriac—the vernacular—which was used inland in order to preserve the Syriac heritage of the Sacred Scriptures and to protect its inherited commentaries and explanations. This status quo remained in effect until the Arab conquest and the geographical and political separation from Byzantium and, consequently the liturgical and hierarchical separation. Actually, this separation took place when the Maronite Patriarchate was created, at the Monastery of Saint Maron, toward the latter part of the seventh century, whereby marking the beginning of the Maronite Liturgical independence.

What has been claimed thus far about the Monastery of Saint Maron and its disciples, or about its movement that took place during the fifth, sixth and seventh centuries, is not a statement that is a biased personal theory without substantial evidence and corroborated proofs. However, the situation herewith does not allow for searching and discussing these documents since such studies are plentiful, widely known and have been published extensively.[11]

During this historical and liturgical period, we believe that the Church Doctrine adopted the Marian teaching of Saint Ephrem which came as a response to Arius and centered around the doctrine of the "Mother of God" in Ephesus. Further, it centered around the unity of the two natures in Christ in Chalcedon and resulted in other theological and moral influences that are mentioned in the writings of the Greek and Syriac Fathers.

2. The Maronite Liturgy:
From Saint John Maron until the Crusades, 700-1100

The Maronite Liturgy is Syriac Antiochene, in many instances, it may be common with the Syriac liturgy and even with the Melkites who gradually abandoned their Antiochene liturgy to adopt the Byzantine's. However, it was the Melkites themselves who started to translate the Byzantine liturgy into Syriac because they were Syrians just like the rest of the inhabitants of Syria; they first adopted the Greek, then later they returned to the Arabic and the Syriac. Melkite manuscripts and Byzantine rituals in Syriac can be counted by the dozens.[12]

Along with many scholars in the field, we believe that in spite of the scarcity of resources during this period, the Maronite Liturgy was not different from the Western Syriac Liturgy, which was quite common with that of the Melkites. It appears, however, that the Maronites have kept their liturgical history closely connected with the Eastern Syriac tradition. Through the *Anaphora* of *Sharrar*, the rituals of the consecration of the Chrism, the hymns in the Liturgy of the Hour and through several letters exchanged between the Maronites and the

[11] Y. Moubarak, *Pentalogie antiochienne*, Beyrouth, 1984, t. 1N1, (pp. 195-275).
[12] C. Charon (C. Karalevsky), *Histoire des Patriarchats melchites*. Rome, 1911, t. III, (pp. 13-14).

Nestorian Patriarch in the eighth century, their Liturgy maintained its closeness to the Eastern Syriac Liturgy.[13]

Therefore, the Marian doctrine of that period and consequently, the Marian Maronite Liturgy was not far from this Syriac tradition. Western Syriac and Jacobites manuscripts, from the seventh to the eleventh century, preserved until today in the libraries of London and Paris, show that they share very many common texts, be it in the *"Sedre"* or in some other hymns. We shall present some of these *Sedre* later, particularly the *Sedro* of the first station of Thursday evening which is dedicated to the Virgin Mary. This same *Sedro* is found in both the Maronite *Sheheemto* and in a Jacobite Syriac manuscript dating back to the seventh or eighth century (British Museum, London, 17129).[14]

3. The Maronite Liturgy:
During the Period of the Crusades, 1100-1300

The Maronite Liturgy remained Syriac Antiochene in nature. It also maintained its dual characteristics of the Eastern and the Western Syriac tradition. In spite of the direct contact with the Crusades and the Roman Liturgy, the letter of Pope Zakhia (Innocent) III in 1215 and the visit of Patriarch Jeremiah Al-Amsheety to Rome to participate in the Fourth Lateran Council which has convened that same year, the Maronite Liturgy did not undergo any changes whatsoever.

No doubt that the special relations between the Maronites and the Crusades, and consequently the Apostolic See, marked the beginning of their Liturgical closeness to the Roman Liturgy. This closeness appeared in the pontifical vestments, the miter, the ring, the consecration of Chrism and the administering of the Sacrament of Confirmation. Further, church art, such as church architecture,

---

[13] -- P. E. Gemayel, *Avant-Messe Maronite Histoire et structure.* Orientalia Christ. anal. 174, Rome 1965, (pp. 202 ss).
  -- R. Bidawid, *The Letters of the Nestorian Patriarch Timothy I,* in *Studi e Testi,* 187 Rome, 1956, (pp. 91 ss).
[14]   Father Youhanna Tabit, *The Divine Office,* Kaslik, 1987, Vol. 2, (pp. 282-283).

mural paintings and sacred vessels, started to infiltrate into the Maronite Church under the influence of the Crusades. But the liturgical texts and the manuscripts of the twelfth and the thirteenth centuries, remained intact in Syriac, witnessing to the fact that they did not undergo the theological "censorship" which affected the liturgical texts of the fifteenth and the sixteenth century, particularly with Eliano and other European delegates.

Consequently, with respect to the Marian doctrine, the Liturgy did not experience any changes or undergo any "Western" influences, in spite of the presence of the Franciscans and the Dominicans among the Maronites.

4. The Maronite Liturgy:
From the end of the period of the Crusades until the Maronite College in Rome, 1300-1584

Historical and written proofs and numerous liturgical manuscripts we possess today, inherited from the time period situated between the thirteenth to the sixteenth century, witness to the fact that the Maronite Liturgical Tradition came from the "treasures of the past," especially where texts, prayers and hymns are concerned. Add to that, the fact that the Jacobite Syriac liturgical tradition penetrated the Maronite territory. After the Crusades, the Jacobites were spread in northern Lebanon and possessed the Syriac cultural power, whereas the Maronites were "persecuted and stranded" between Lebanon and Cyprus.

Due to the arrival of European Missionaries among the Maronites, especially before and after the Council of Florence, some Western liturgical customs and theological thoughts began to slowly settle in. After the return of the Maronite Franciscan, Gabriel Iben Al-Qala'ee from Rome in 1494, where he spent around twenty years learning philosophy and theology, he started spreading among the Maronites the translated contemporary Latin theological thoughts. Iben Al-Qala'ee, and his students after him, incorporated many Latin liturgical texts and traditions. The "latinization" process had not yet occurred. However, if any took place, it was very limited due to the paucity of "manuscripts" and to the fact that these manuscripts were neither well accepted nor widely published.

The "Rosary" may have been gradually introduced to the Maronites toward the end of this historical period, along with some Franciscan devotions and hymns, coming from Rome and entering into Mount Lebanon via the Holy Land. Bear in mind that the Jacobite influence was very strong during the sixteenth century whereby their literature and manuscripts were spreading among the Maronites in northern Lebanon.[15]

5. The Maronite Liturgy:
From the Maronite College in Rome and the Printing of Liturgical Books until Patriarch Stephen Al-Douwayhi, 1584-1670

After Father Eliano had visited the Maronites in 1578 he was enraged about the number of "Jacobite" books he found in their hands. Upon his return to Rome he suggested that necessary measures must be taken to provide them with a proper "Catholic education" and to rectify their theological books. He further suggested instituting a press in order to publish liturgical and spiritual books and to establish a College in Rome to graduate Maronite priests highly trained and educated in theology.

The wishes of Father Eliano were granted. The press started in 1580, the College opened in 1584 and the printing of the liturgical books "as corrected" was launched. The funeral book was printed in 1585, the Missal in 1594, the Lectionary in 1596, the *Sheheemto* in 1624 along with the book of feast days, the winter *Fenqitho* in 1656 and the summer *Fenqitho* in 1666.

The graduates of this College were divided with regard to the printing of these books and with the concerns that this may cause the "latinization" of the Liturgy. After the Patriarch and the bishops had refused the use of the first Missal printed in 1594, they later accepted the text but only temporarily, upon the advice of Father Dandini in 1596. Following the revolt of some Maronites against this western current, Gerges A'mayra, who later became the Patriarch, refused to approve any Episcopal ordination ceremony except the one that was

---

[15] Michael Al-Raggi, *The Maronite Ritual*, in Almashriq, Beirut, 1935, (pp. 481-522).

printed in the Latin Pontifical. We need not emphasize that during this historical period numerous devotions, many of which are Marian, started to take shape gradually.

6. Patriarch Stephen Al-Douwayhi, 1670-1704

Patriarch Stephen Al-Douwayhi is a notable landmark in the history of Maronite Rituals. He was a great figure who studied the liturgical books and organized them according to the authentic Maronite Tradition. Given the very limited resources at the time, by gathering ancient Maronite manuscripts and studying them closely, he was able to define the parameters of the liturgical heritage. He rectified most of the rituals; he published and distributed them once again among the Maronites in order to reclaim the true liturgical origins. There is no need to list all the articles he prepared for publication because they encompass the majority of the rituals. His main concern was to rid the liturgical books, as much as he possibly could, from the Jacobite and the Latin components. Popes as well as high ranking officials in Rome accepted his proposed reform with very little modification, which was translated into Latin and prepared to be published. Unfortunately, the Patriarch died "before his eyes could see any of these books published."

7. The Synod of Mount Lebanon, 1736 and Subsequent Synods, 1755 and 1756

One could not find in these synods any "special legislation" for liturgical rituals as we have recently experienced in the Second Vatican Council. But each and every one of these synods commanded the return to the authenticity of the Maronite Liturgy, to the necessity of reform and to publish liturgical books with extreme care of competent liturgical committees guided by the Patriarch. Details regarding the reform and the return to the authentic tradition are quite numerous. It is commonly known that the "latinization" process of the rituals after the reform of Patriarch Al-Douwayhi increased when it was supposed to decrease.

Published books of the eighteenth and the nineteenth centuries witness to this fact, some of which are listed as follows:

- The Book of Rituals, along with the Service of the Mysteries and some blessings, published in Rome in 1752, is a direct translation from the Latin Ritual.

- The Book of "Rituals" called also the seasonal rituals the devotional services and several others, published in Rome in 1839 and reprinted in 1909, is presently in liturgical use.

- As for the Marian devotions and other liturgical services, this book consists of what we have at the present time, such as the devotion of the Rosary, the service of the Scapular of our Lady and many other... Latin services!

Conclusion

The Second Vatican Council issued a decree on the Liturgy which emphasized the respect of the Eastern Liturgies and the necessity of returning to the origins of their particular Tradition. This decree actually caused a liturgical revolution in the West and encouraged Eastern Churches to delve into their own Liturgies, to reform them and return them into their authentic origins. This encouragement came from high ranking officials in the Roman Curia, who insisted on returning to the rich Eastern Tradition, to its Fathers and to its spirituality.

The liturgical revolution, caused by the Second Vatican Council, has actually prompted the writing of this book about the Virgin Mary in the history of the Maronite Liturgy. It has inspired us to return, not only to the period of the Crusaders, but also to the period which has preceded the tenth century wherein we shall experience a common Antiochene Syriac Maronite Tradition. This tradition is found in the Marian feasts, in the texts of the liturgical prayers, in the *Qurbono* and in the devotional service of the icon of the Virgin Mary. This is what shall be explored next.

CHAPTER VI

Mary in the Maronite Liturgical Year: Her Feasts and Memorials

The liturgical year plays a significant role in the life of the Maronite community, especially the way in which the Christian faith is lived. Since Christianity is based on salvation through Jesus Christ, it projects his face as Savior in the various stages of salvation and places him on a salvific journey and plan from the beginning of Creation until the end of time.

The most important stations of salvation are as follows:

- The creation of the first man, Adam, his fall, then the promise of salvation

- The emplacement of humanity on the road to salvation through the covenant that God made with the people of the Old Testament and the preparation for the coming of Christ the Savior

- The Incarnation, the Proclamation, and the Redemption through Death and Resurrection

- The descent of the Holy Spirit and the beginning of the mission by the Church

- The Church is the visible body of Christ. She lives and preaches until salvation is complete by encountering Christ at the end of the world.

This is the divine plan for the salvation of man through Christ. The place of the Virgin Mary in this plan is notable, multifaceted and in complete harmony. Thus, when the Maronite Liturgy lives these stations of salvation, she lives them with the Virgin Mary through the various symbols which the Church has established about her. The Virgin Mary is the woman through whom salvation was complete for "Christ was born from a woman" who is the second Eve, the new Eve, from whose lineage comes the Savior, who will crush the head of the serpent. She is the Virgin Mother about whom the prophets foretold and from whom "Emmanuel" shall be born.

Therefore, the Maronite Liturgy lives the events that are connected with the period that precedes the coming of the Savior which consists of seven Sundays: the first is dedicated to the Church and the other six are known by the Sundays of the Season of Announcements.

The two notable feasts dedicated to the Virgin Mary are the first two Sundays of the Season of Announcements: the Sunday of the Angel's Announcement to Mary and the Sunday of the Visitation of Mary to Elizabeth. These two feasts link the Old Testament to the New Testament: In the Announcement to Mary in Nazareth, the Angel came announcing the Good News and the prophecies were fulfilled: "The virgin will conceive and will bear a son who will be called Emmanuel." Mary takes this Good News to Elizabeth who is expecting one of the Old—New Testament prophets John, while Elizabeth proclaims: "Through you, O Mary, all the promises and the covenants were fulfilled, you are full of grace, O mother of my Lord!"

With these two feasts, the Annunciation and the Visitation..., we begin our Maronite liturgical year right after the commemoration of the Church. Following these two feasts the preparatory events of Christmas begin to unfold. First, we learn of the birth of John and how the angel dissipates the doubt that Joseph had in the spotless Mother. Second, we learn about the royal genealogy beginning with Abraham and ending with "Joseph the spouse of Mary from whom Jesus, who is called the Christ, is born." Then "she gave birth to her first-born Son," the light glistened, the angels sang and the caravan of those who came to congratulate Mary arrived.

In the Liturgy also, those who are bringing good wishes come the day after Christmas, whereby the Church celebrates the feast of the Praises of the Mother of God, congratulating her on the birth of her divine child, praising her divine motherhood and the loftiness of her place. Thus, with the Blessed Virgin Mary, we live the Mystery of the Incarnation.

In the Maronite Liturgy, the season of the Great Lent is the period during which the proclamation of the faith begins. In the Liturgy, as in the Gospel of John, it begins with the miracle of Cana, the first Sunday of Lent, where the Virgin Mary is present in this Lenten Season and culminates with the Mystery of Redemption through Christ's death and resurrection. The Maronite Liturgy lives this period with the "Sorrowful Mother" who is standing by the Cross; and at the very first joyful ringing of bells announcing the joy of the Resurrection we proclaim: "Mary, weep no more, for Christ is truly risen."

As Maronites we live the Mystery of Redemption, which is immersed in the life of the Virgin Mary from the Incarnation and Redemption, to the launching of the Church in the upper room, where Mary was with the **Apostles,** and where the face of Mary, the Mother of God and the Mother of the Church, clearly shines forth.

The Maronite Church lives its rituals, **after Pentecost and the feast of the Apostles,** in the liturgical season of Our Lady, on August 15, which is the greatest Marian feast at the present time. It is the feast of her Dormition and of her Assumption into heaven—a feast of great importance just like all other great liturgical feasts. In preparation for the feast, the Maronite Church starts the fast, the offering of sacrifices and prayers in the beginning of August, or two weeks prior to its celebration. For the celebration of this feast, the Church has reserved its greatest and most important celebration. The Maronite Tradition notes that, when the apostles gathered from all directions of the world for her Assumption, they celebrated the Eucharistic Liturgy according to the *Anaphora* of *Sharrar*, which is known to be the oldest Maronite *anaphora*.

According to the Maronite liturgical year, the stages of salvation are accomplished with the feast of the Exaltation of the Cross, which points to the end of the world. It culminates through the victory of the triumphant Cross by extinguishing the human flame on earth, which was ignited with creation in paradise.

The major feast days of the Virgin Mary are: the Annunciation, the Visitation, the Praises of the Mother of God, the day after Christmas, her sharing in the Passion, Death, Resurrection and Pentecost, then her Assumption through the anticipation of the final coming.

Therefore, a clear understanding of the feasts and memorials of the Virgin Mary is characterized as follows:

1. The old feasts, closely connected with the liturgical cycle, are most often shared between all the Eastern Churches. For example: the feast of her divine motherhood.

2. The memorials are more recent than the feasts and are related to special events in her life. For example: her conception, her birthday, her presentation to the Temple, then of course, the memorials of the plantations, the harvest and the grapes...

3. The feasts that penetrated the Maronite Calendar under the influence of the Roman Calendar started either during the seventeenth or the eighteenth century. For example: the feast of the Holy Rosary...

4. In addition to these feasts and memorials there are some special "months" of the year, "days" of the week, and "hours" of the day that are called "Marian."

1. The Old Feasts of the Virgin Mary connected with the Liturgical Year

The oldest feast is the one which is linked to the divine Incarnation and the birth of the Word. This feast is known today as the feast of the Praises of the Virgin Mary and is celebrated the day after Christmas. Thus, the Church connected the closest person to the Incarnation, who is the Virgin Mary, to the great event of salvation. Therefore, the feast was known from the earliest days of the Church as the feast of the "Mother of God" or the feast of the "Praises of the Mother of God." This feast, which is bringing congratulations to the

"Mother of God" and to the Church, is connected to two other feasts closely related to the preparation of Christmas and commemorated through two important events: the Annunciation of the angel to the Virgin Mary and the Visitation of Mary to Elizabeth.

From an historical standpoint, it is safe to claim that the feast of the "Mother of God" developed in the fifth century after the Council of Ephesus, while the other two feasts found their place in the Liturgical Year, at its final development, before the eighth century. As for the old memorial which started in local churches venerating her and later spread to the rest of the churches, following the Ecumenical Councils, it is in fact the feast of her "Dormition," or the date which commemorates her Assumption on August 15. This feast may have developed quite early in the Church around her tomb in Jerusalem and spread later to the various "Marian churches" until it was officially promulgated by Emperor Mauricius in the year 600 and by the Pope shortly thereafter.

The feast of the Dormition of the Virgin Mary "which is one of the greatest Marian feasts" among all the Eastern Churches, even in the Nestorian Church, is preceded by a one-week or two-week fast while the celebration of the feast itself extends up to two weeks in order to complete the festivities. Furthermore, this is a very special feast in the Maronite Church. The Patriarch used to celebrate the *Qurbono* with the greatest number of clergy and laity attending. The *Anaphora* of "*Sharrar*," known as the *Anaphora* of the "Apostles," is used during this celebration as it has been mentioned earlier. The prayers are alternated between the Patriarch, who represents Peter, and the bishops who represent the rest of the Apostles.[16] Father Eliano described the celebration of this feast of Our Lady in Qannoubeen on August 15, in 1580 saying:

> "Throughout the eve of the feast, people from all different regions flocked to Qannoubeen. The Patriarch and those who have already arrived, watched from the monastery rooftop the throngs of people who are still coming. Meanwhile, church bells ring, peasants fuel bonfires and light fireworks. Others discharge firearms while peoples' jubilation and shouts of joy

---

[16] Refer to the Manuscripts of this *Anaphora* in *The Maronite Mass,* 1970, (p. 185).

escalate! On the day of the feast itself everyone shares in the celebration of the Pontifical *Qurbono*, bishops, clergy and the entire assembly."[17]

2. The Special Marian Memorials

Along with the development of the Marian devotions and the spread of the apocryphal gospels which talked at great length about the life of the Virgin Mary, three feasts appeared related to her conception, her birth and her presentation at the Temple. In the East, since the sixth century, there developed the feast of Anna who conceived Mary on December 9, the feast of Mary's birth on September 8, and the feast of her presentation at the Temple on November 21 when she was three years old.

Up until the sixth century, therefore, the feasts and the memorials of the Virgin Mary were recognized in the East as follows:

- The memorial before Christmas became later the feast of the Annunciation of the angel to the Virgin Mary

- The feast of Mary's conception on December 9, which is nine months before her birth

- The feast of her birth on September 8

- The feast of her Dormition and Assumption on August 15.

The feasts of Mary's divine motherhood and the feast of the Praises of the Mother of God were most likely added around the fifth century. The Annunciation on March 25, nine months before the birth of Jesus, was added as early as the fifth or the sixth century. Three other feasts surfaced around the Antiochene surrounding since that date: the feast of Our Lady of plantations on January 15; the feast of Our Lady of the harvest on May 15; and the feast of our Lady of the grapes on August 15. These feasts may have been of pagan origin dedicated to the gods of plantation, of harvest and of grapes long before Christianity.

---

[17] Father Gilbert, *"The Virgin Mary in Lebanon,"* (pp. 214, 296).

Another local feast entered the picture, which is the finding of the veil and the cincture of the Virgin Mary on July 2. It may have been originally a dedicating memorial for a prominent Church named after the Virgin Mary.

These were the common Maronite feasts shared with the Byzantine and the West Syriac Churches. As for the East Syriac Churches, the Nestorians have four memorials:

- The Annunciation is on a Sunday that precedes Christmas
- The Praises of the Virgin Mary is the day after Christmas
- Our Lady of plantations and of the harvest is on May 15
- The Dormition is on August 15.

3. The Maronite Feasts of Western Origins

Three major Marian feasts in the Maronite Calendar have originated in the West:

A. The feast of Our Lady of the Rosary is celebrated on October 7. The Sunday of the Rosary, (the month of the Rosary), is one of the feasts of the Latin calendar. It was initially celebrated by the Dominican Order and then instituted by Pope Pius V to give thanks to the Virgin Mary for having delivered Christendom from the Turks by the decisive sea battle of "Lepanto" which took place on October 7, 1571. It was later promulgated by Pope Clement XI as an official feast for the entire Church in 1716. It reached the Maronites in the eighteenth century and officially entered the Maronite Book of Rituals which was printed in Rome in 1839.

B. The feast of Our Lady of Carmel is celebrated on July 16 by the Carmelite monks and was later promulgated by the Pope as an official feast for the entire church in 1726. It reached the Maronite devotions in the eighteenth century and became quite popular because of the "scapular" which was connected with this devotion. It also made its way to the Maronite Book of Rituals which was printed in Rome in 1839.

C.   The feast of the Visitation is on July 2. However, this special commemoration is known in the Syriac and the Byzantine East, not as the feast of the Visitation, but as the feast of the finding of the veil and the cincture of the Virgin Mary. This feast reached the Latin Calendar through the Franciscans since the fifteenth century, which actually falls one week after the birth of John the Baptizer on June 24. It entered the Maronite Calendar in the eighteenth century.

4. The Marian Months, Days and Hours

In the present Maronite Calendar, Mary is honored in a special way during the months of August, October and May:

- One week before and one week after the actual feast day which falls on August 15

- October is dedicated to honor the Holy Rosary

- May, the entire month, is the "Month of Mary."

The history of these three months is as follows:

The Month of August. The feast of the Assumption is the greatest feast of the Virgin Mary which takes place on August 15. In the entire East it is preceded by two weeks of prayer, abstinence and fasting in preparation for the feast day during which the faithful frequent the Church to honor the Blessed Mother through hymns and prayers. Some Maronite liturgical books mention special prayers and chants dedicated for the Sunday that follows the feast of the Assumption. Nearly, the entire month is dedicated to the Virgin Mary, without necessarily following a monthly, but rather a weekly cycle.

The Month of October. As mentioned above, the history of the month of October and the Holy Rosary started in the seventeenth century. It was officially promulgated as the month of the Holy Rosary in the Catholic Church in the eighteenth century and was finally published in our liturgical books and became quite popular among our devotions in the nineteenth century.

The Month of May. This month is a fairly recent import to Lebanon. It found its way in with the second wave of Jesuits around 1833 where the icon of the Virgin Mary was placed in the Church of Our Lady of Deliverance in the monastery of the Jesuit Fathers in Bikfaya. This unknown devotion, at the time, spread all over Lebanon by dedicating the month of May to the Virgin Mary. Through the direction of the Jesuits, the Marian sororities have had a great involvement in spreading this devotion during the month of May.

The Days and the Hours

The *liturgical day* in which we honor the Virgin Mary is Wednesday because it is the day of her "Dormition." This is a common Eastern tradition dating back to the sixth or the seventh century. As for the *liturgical hour* that is dedicated to honor the Virgin Mary in the Maronite Prayer of the Hours, it is the first station of the midnight prayer. Furthermore, Mary's Canticle, "My soul magnifies the Lord" is included among many other lengthy songs and hymns in every Morning Prayer.

It is not surprising that, in every Syriac melody, in all the prayers and in all the Maronite services, there is a special strophe dedicated to the Virgin Mary. It comes after the psalm and it is usually the third of four strophes of that particular hymn.

For all of these feasts and memorials the Virgin Mary there are prayers and hymns some of which are old and some are new. There is also a special commemoration in the Qurbono, in the Mysteries, in the liturgical services, particularly in the Benediction with the icon of the Virgin Mary on her feast days and memorials. This is what shall be explored next in details.

CHAPTER VII

Mary in the Maronite Liturgical Prayer

In the Maronite Church, the communal liturgical prayer is recited seven times daily. The prayer begins in the evening, according to the liturgical formula concluding the day with the sunset and beginning the next day immediately after sundown. This is the liturgical prayer which is known as the "Divine Office" and consists of the following seven liturgical prayers:

1. The Evening Prayer takes place at sundown.
2. The Night Prayer takes place before going to bed.
3. The Midnight Prayer consists of four different stations.
4. The Morning Prayer takes place at sunrise.
5. The Prayer of the Third Hour takes place at nine o'clock in the morning.
6. The Prayer of the Sixth Hour takes place at noon.
7. The Prayer of the Ninth Hour takes place at three o'clock in the afternoon.

These seven daily prayers consist of various psalms, hymns and petitions to which were added readings from the Sacred Scriptures. Initially, they were written in Syriac and distributed among all liturgical feast days, most of the Sundays and a number of devotional services. These prayers are preserved in Maronite liturgical books, the majority of which is published. The most popular book is the "*Sheheemto*" which contains the common prayers used during the ordinary days and Sundays. The *Fenqitho* book, however, contains the liturgical feast days and Sundays, while the *Teshmeshto* book is mostly for the holy days of obligations and the memorials, of which a good number of these books are still in manuscript form.

These prayers number approximately one hundred multiplied by seven, because there are seven liturgical prayers for every feast. Add to that the numerous Marian feasts, to each of these there are seven prayers, all of which are dedicated to honor the Virgin Mary.

It may be impossible to go into all these Marian texts of the liturgical prayers. It is just as difficult to give a definite date to each of these prayers and hymns. We are not about to furnish baseless opinions about the Maronite Marian theology without having first acquired historical evidence and direct contact with these texts. Therefore, we have chosen a collection of basic Marian prayers and a sample of hymns from their Syriac sources, to express, even literally, the Maronite Marian thoughts that are embedded in our liturgical texts. Each text has its history and peculiarity, thus a separate introduction is provided for each of them. However, a summary of the Maronite Syriac Marian theological thought is explored in detail in chapter ten.

We should like to clarify that the provided texts are the actual texts of the Maronite liturgical books which, in fact, are in use at the present time. Even if most of these texts date back to the period preceding the tenth century, most of them may have been shared with the Syriac Antiochene Liturgy in general and with the Western Syriac Liturgy in particular.

These are the introductions to each particular text:

1. The Sunday Prayer

It is the fourth *Sedro* which is mentioned in the first station of the Sunday prayer and published in the 1890 Beirut Edition of the *"Sheheemto"* (pp. 47-48). This is the same S*edro* which is found in the liturgy of the word in the present Maronite *Qurbono* in the 1908 Beirut Edition. The *Sedro,* or the *Hoosoyo,* as we know it today, is a basic prayer in the Divine Office which constitutes the "theological thought" of the feast accompanied by the imposing of the penitential incense. These prayers exist among the Western Syriac tradition, the Maronites and the Melkites, but it is not known among the

Chaldeans. It may have been the Jacobite Patriarch, known as John "Sedrawy" among those who first organized this type of prayers around the year 648.

For this topic consult the following sources:

- J. Mateos, (in French) *"Sedre et prieres connues dans quelques anciennes collections"* or *"Sedre and common prayers in several ancient collections."* Orient. Christ. Per. XXVIII, 1962, (pp. 239-287)

- Boutros Gemayel, (in Arabic) *"al quddas al marouni"* or *"The Maronite Mass"* 1970, (pp. 129-133)

- Youhanna Tabit, (in Arabic) *"al fardh al elahi"* or *"The Divine Office"* Kaslik, 1987, New Lights on the Maronite Divine Office, (pp. 257-268).

Regarding this *Sedro*, we did not find any types in the non-Maronite Syriac texts comparable to it that might be dedicated to the Virgin Mary. This does not mean that it is exclusively "Maronite," but it is widely used in the Maronite *Qurbono* and the Divine Office to the point where it had become the "main Marian *Sedro*." In fact, it completely expresses the troubled life of the Maronite who petitions the Virgin Mary from the recesses of his soul because of the pain and suffering he endures. It dates back to the period that precedes the tenth century.

2. The Monday Prayer

The *Sedro* is chosen from the first station of the Monday Night Prayer and published in the 1908 Beirut Edition of the *Sheheemto* (pp. 214-216). It is characterized by emphasizing that the Virgin Mary deserves the title of "Mother of God." It also lavishes upon her the title of "intercessor for the influence she has with her Son..." This *Sedro* further stresses the acquisition of strong love and true faith. It dates back to either the seventh or the eighth century.

3. The Tuesday Prayer

The *Sedro* is chosen from the first station of the Tuesday Night Prayer and published in the 1908 Beirut Edition of the *Sheheemto* (pp. 277-280). There is a high and lofty description of the rank that the Virgin Mary has attained: "He raised the lowly to high places." We call her blessed and with all nations we glorify her from age to age. It dates back to the period that precedes the tenth century.

4. The Wednesday Prayer

The *Sedro* is chosen from the first station of the Wednesday Night Prayer and published in the 1908 Beirut Edition of the *Sheheemto* (pp. 340-343). It is alphabetically organized. The successive descriptions which occur in the prayer about the attributes of Jesus (the Lord God, the Son of Mary) do follow the alphabetical order, for example: A stands for Ancient..., B for beautiful..., E for Eternal..., S for Savior..., and so forth. This type of poetic writing is very common in the *Sheheemto,* more of which is found in the "Divine Office" published by Youhanna Tabit in 1987, (pp. 258-259). This *Sedro* summarizes the praises of the Mother of God and magnifies her blessedness because she became the Mother of God whose attributes are numerous. It dates back to the period that precedes the tenth century.

5. The Thursday Prayer

The *Sedro* is chosen from the first station of the Thursday Night Prayer and published in the 1908 Beirut Edition of the *Sheheemto* (pp. 418-420). At the present time it is preserved in the British Museum in London, in the manuscript collection of 170129. It dates back to either the seventh or the eighth century. For further details regarding this *Sedro*, you may consult the previous references of J. Mateos and Father Youhanna Tabit. The basic theological thought of this *Sedro* centers around Mary "the Mother of God" for she fulfilled the prophecies and walked the journey of salvation, thus, she became "loftier than the heavens." Ultimately, she intercedes for us so that we may walk the true Christian path. This is one of the oldest and most beautiful *Sedro* ever written.

6. The Friday Prayer

The *Sedro* is chosen from the first station of the Friday Night Prayer and published in the 1908 Beirut Edition of the *Sheheemto* (pp. 476-479). It is a prayer to Christ who "dwelt in the womb of the Virgin who was sanctified in body and soul through the gifts of the Holy Spirit," in order to sustain the Church and her children through the intercession of His Mother. There are many attributes of the outstanding beauty of the Virgin Mary and, at the same time, there are popular petitions stemming from the needs of the faithful. It dates back to the period that precedes the tenth century.

7. The Saturday Prayer

The *Sedro* is chosen from the first station of the Saturday Night Prayer and published in the 1908 Beirut Edition of the *Sheheemto* (pp. 557-559). This *Sedro* embodies deep theological thought about the Mystery of the Incarnation such as "He took flesh from you and divinized us" and "He became poor and enriched us." There are also some Eastern Syriac thoughts on meditation known as "intellectual meditations." It dates back to the period that precedes the tenth century.

8. The Annunciation Prayer

The Sunday Morning *Sedro* of the Annunciation is taken from the *Fenqitho*, which was published in Rome in 1656. It may belong to an old manuscript that we were not able to study closely, but it is preserved with the old Maronite collection of manuscripts in Bkerke/Deman referring either to the twelfth or the thirteenth century. The *Sedro* dates back to the period that precedes the tenth century. This text is published in the *Prayer of the Faithful,* by Boutros Gemayel, Volume I, (pp. 312-313).

The Annunciation takes us back to Paradise and the first fall so we may see in Jesus a second Adam and in Mary a second Eve.

9. The Visitation Prayer

The Sunday Morning *Sedro* of the Visitation is taken from the *Fenqitho,* which was published in Rome in 1656. It may belong to an old Maronite collection of manuscripts from either the twelfth or the thirteenth century and preserved in Bkerke/Deman. The *Sedro* itself dates back to the period that precedes the tenth century. This text is published in the *Prayer of the Faithful,* by Boutros Gemayel, Volume I, (p. 351).

The basic thought is: Today, the prophecies were fulfilled. Today, the "One who is full of grace," as she carried Jesus, visited "John the forerunner" and he was sanctified.

10. The Assumption Prayer

The *Sedro* of the Night Prayer (prayer before going to bed) of the feast of the Assumption is taken from the *Fenqitho,* which was published in Rome in 1666. It may also belong to the old Collection of the Maronite Manuscripts. The date of this manuscript could not be determined! This *Sedro* hints to the tradition that resulted from the apocryphal gospels recounting that the Apostles gathered from all directions of the earth to bid farewell to the Blessed Virgin. The reference to the places of the world where the Apostles preached has a deep conviction of faith.

11. A Hymn from the Sunday Morning Prayer

This is the third *Fsheeto* tune, which is the third before the last strophe. It is chosen from the Sunday Morning Prayer and published in the 1908 Beirut Edition of the *Sheheemto* (p. 138). This text can also be found in the above mentioned reference of Father Youhanna Tabit (p. 281). This hymn mentions the three Marian feasts of January, May and August, connects them to the agricultural feasts and gives them a "universal" meaning taking them back to Saint John and to Ephesus! It is based on a Johannine apocryphal "revelation" about the Virgin Mary.

12. *Sooghyoto* of the Virgin Mary

This hymn is composed after the *Sooghito* style, and dedicated for the Morning celebration of the feast of the Rosary. It is available in Syriac along with its Arabic translation in the current Maronite *Book of Rituals* which was printed in 1909 (pp. 266-269). "It is sung with the clanging of cymbals"! It lists the Praises of the Virgin Mary with a brief history of all the Church Fathers who glorified her. This hymn further mentions the Antiochene, the Byzantine and the Syriac Fathers along with a special mention of Saint "Maron." While the Arabic translation reads "Maron who nourished his children" it adds "the inhabitants of Lebanon," the Syriac translation reads "and Maron nourished his children" (from the milk of your virginity). Further, the Syriac version mentions the "Lebanese Zephyrinus," whereas the Arabic version deleted the term "Lebanese" (the fourth line).

These *Sooghyoto* list all the heresies committed against the Virgin Mary and mentions the Church Fathers who renounced them. They are known to be both Maronite as well as Melkite *Sooghyoto*, but their dates are unknown.

1. The Sunday Prayer

Proemion

May we offer praise, glory and honor to the exalted One, who humbled himself and exalted the humble Virgin; to the Lord, who became flesh and saved the human race; to the Most High, who lowered himself and raised up the lowly; the Good One to whom are due glory and honor, now and forever.

People: Amen.

Sedro

As we praise and glorify with spiritual hymns, the Blessed Ever-Virgin Mary, Mother of God, we ask her to petition the fruit of her womb, for us saying:

O Lord, through the prayers of your Mother, keep away from the earth and all its inhabitants the scourge of wrath; eliminate dangers and disturbances; remove from us wars, captivity, hunger and plague. Have compassion on us, we are weak; comfort us, we are sick; assist us, we are poor; deliver us, we are oppressed; grant rest to the faithful departed who have left us and grant us a peaceful death so that we raise glory to You now, at all times, and forever.

People: Amen.

2. The Monday Prayer

Proemion

May we offer praise, glory and honor to the Holy One who sanctified the Virgin who conceived him; to the Most High who exalted the humble Virgin who nursed him; to the glorified One who honored the pure Virgin who venerated him; the Good One to whom are due glory and honor, now and forever.

People: Amen.

Sedro

O powerful Word of God, we celebrate the plan of salvation you accomplished for our sake, and honor the memory of the Blessed Virgin, your Mother, adorned with purity and worthy of being Mother of God. She is our pride because she afforded us life and brought us salvation.

About her spoke the Fathers and the Patriarchs. Through her the promises of the prophets and saints were fulfilled. Thus, she became the pride of the Law and the Prophets, the honor of the Apostles, the refuge of the weak and the consolation of the oppressed, because she alone has earned your favor and never returned disappointed since she is the Mother of God.

Through her and with her, the pure one, we offer You our petitions and supplications on the day of her memorial. In your love, free us from temptation and grant us happy days and peaceful times so that you may strengthen our love for you and each other. Unite us through the belt of the true faith and honor your flock which was saved by your divine saving passion, so that we may glorify the memory of the Virgin Mary. With her and with all the saints who have prophesied about her from the beginning, grant us to reach the heavenly dwelling places of light so that, along with our departed, we may be spared the final judgment. Therefore, we all shall offer glory to You, to your Father and to your Holy Spirit, forever.

People: Amen.

3. The Tuesday Prayer

Proemion

May we offer praise, glory and honor to the ever-vigilant One whose light never ceases and whom the angels constantly worship; to the Light Who is praised unceasingly by the heavenly hosts who are illumined by Him; to the Word of God, One person of the Holy Trinity, the Son Who is one in being with the Father and glorified by divine powers; the One who lowered himself, dwelt in the pure Virgin Mary and, in his compassion, saved our human race; the Good One to whom are due glory and honor, now and forever.

People: Amen.

Sedro

Who can count the praises of the Blessed Virgin Mary? She became a highly fortified mountain to receive the power of God and His Word; she became loftier than the chariot depicted by Daniel, because she carried God in his divine and human natures. She is the paradise of the second Adam and the bush that was never consumed by the divine power! She is the one who was adorned with all the beauties of holiness through the indwelling of the Holy Spirit!

> She is the second heaven in whom the Sun of the world dwelt in the flesh!

> She is the meek ewe, from whom was born the Shepherd of shepherds, the Lamb of God who bears the sins of the world!

She is the Mother of the Light who, through His birth, has enlightened the world and dissipated all darkness!

She is the Virgin Mother who became the Mother of God Incarnate, who paid off the debt of Adam, our first father. As she became the Mother of God, while remaining a holy virgin, we adorn her, just as she prophesied, and petition her saying:

> Blessed are you Mary, because you became the Mother of the One who, through his wisdom, created heaven and separated the land from the seas.
> The Prophets bless you, because through you, their prophecies were fulfilled.
> The Apostles bless you, because you became the cause for their preaching.
> The Martyrs and Confessors bless you, because you are the pride of their struggle and crowns.
> The Fathers and Doctors of the Church bless you, because you silenced the voices of heresies by being the Mother of the Incarnate One!

And now we petition you, O Christ our God, through the prayers of your Mother and your Saints: look with compassion upon us and accept our offerings and supplications upon your altar; grant, O Lord, healing to the sick, consolation to the sufferings, guidance to the faltering, good hope to the living and eternal rest to the departed. As for us, your weak and poor servants, enable us to repent so that we may become pure and chaste, serene and peaceful. Grant us to celebrate your feasts with joy and happiness, all the days of our lives, so that we may reach eternal life, where we shall offer glory to You, to Your Father and to Your Holy Spirit, forever.

People: Amen.

4. The Wednesday Prayer

Proemion

May we offer praise, glory and honor to the Blessed Fruit Who appeared from the Virgin Mary and gave life to those who have died after they have eaten the forbidden fruit; to the Blessed Son Who glorified the memory of His Mother and exalted her feast above all other feasts; the Good One to whom are due glory and honor, now and forever.

People: Amen.

Sedro

Who can possibly simplify the praises of the Blessed Virgin Mary, the Mother of God who is full of grace! She is the one whom Isaiah called the "Virgin Mother of Emmanuel." She is the one whom the Gospel called "Blessed among women." She is the fleece who accepted the dew from Heaven and of whom was born the Most Holy whose star has shone for the Magi. She is the one whom the prophet called the cloud who carried the One who could not be carried. She is the one from whom the bright light has shone upon us from the bosom of the Father, the One who dwells in the heavens and the Savior of the world!

As we sing to her the hymns of the Holy Spirit, we petition her saying:

>Blessed are you, because you became the mother of the Eternal One who is begotten from the Father.
>Blessed are you, because you became the mother of the Creator who created all things, seen and unseen.
>Blessed are you, because you became the mother of the One Who is hidden and unknown.
>Blessed are you, because you became the mother of the One Who guided us to the dwellings of light and joy.
>Blessed are you, because you became the mother of the One Who is the sea of extraordinary love for mankind.
>Blessed are you, because you became the mother of the One Who made us children and heirs of the Heavenly Kingdom.
>Blessed are you, because you became the mother of the One Who is compassionate and does not know anger.
>Blessed are you, because you became the mother of the Merciful God whose compassion is extended to all.
>Blessed are you, because you became the mother of the only Light who is one person of the Holy Trinity.

Blessed are you, because you became the mother of the true Hope who never deceives through His honest promises.

Blessed are you, because you became the mother of the One Who dawned from the bosom of the Father before all times and creation.

Blessed are you, because you became the mother of the One Who calls the dead from the grave and raises sinners from their rut.

Blessed are you, because you became the mother of the Mighty One whose glory has filled heaven and earth.

And now, O Lord, as we celebrate her feast with blessedness and praises, we petition her to intercede for us so that, some day, we may stand without blemish before your judgment seat. Make us worthy, along with our departed and all those who died in the true faith, to reach the dwelling places of happiness where we shall offer glory to You, to Your Father and to Your Holy Spirit, now and forever.

People: Amen.

5. The Thursday Prayer

Proemion

May we offer praise, glory and honor to the First-born of the Eternal Father, Who was born of the Virgin in due time; to the hidden One Who became visible and appeared from the Blessed Virgin Mary! The Good One to whom are due glory and honor, now and forever.

People: Amen.

Sedro

O Jesus Christ, Lord of all, Our God and Savior, Who for our salvation, You humbled yourself to become one of us. You dwelt in the womb of the Virgin, which was sanctified by the Holy Spirit, the womb of your Mother, the Blessed Virgin Mary who is without blemish; not as the heresy claims, because she is truly the Mother of God!

She is higher than the heavens!

She is the one who received the greeting from Archangel Gabriel when he told her: the Lord is with you and from you He will appear, you, who are blessed among women.

She is the one who received the gifts from the Magi and the Shepherds in Bethlehem.

She is the one who became the blessed vine who gave the grape of blessedness and forgiveness to those who drank His wine.

She is the one who alone was called "Mother of God" by the saintly Prophets who served the divine mysteries.

She is the one who, exalted above all creation, has earned the supreme favor from the One who was born from her.

O Lord, You who willed to take flesh from her and became human for our sake, grant us peace and tranquility through her prayers. Keep away from us visible and invisible wars. Enlighten us with the gift of the true faith which is acceptable to you. Grant us peaceful times that may befitting our journey. Command that our souls possess genuine and unwavering love. Make us strangers to all kind of lies and deceit. Instill within us a reputable life which may not cause slander against your Holy Name. Heal us from the sickness of soul and body. Forgive the sins of those who distinguished themselves by honoring the feast of your pure and blessed Mother. Sustain our lives and theirs from temptation and deadly sin and imbue them with noble deeds. Grant us and our departed to behold your smiling face on the Day of Judgment when we shall offer glory to You, to Your Father and to Your Holy Spirit, forever.

People: Amen.

6. The Friday Prayer

Proemion

May we offer praise, glory and honor to the Eternal and Celestial One Who came to us from the Ever-bright Light; to the beautiful aroma and the sweet fragrance Who leads to God the Father; to the One Who, in due time, appeared from the Blessed Mother; to the One Who glorified the memory of His Mother, the Blessed Virgin Mary; the Good One to whom are due glory and honor, now and forever.

People: Amen.

Sedro

O Christ, power and wisdom of God the Father; O King of kings and creator of all; for our salvation, You humbled yourself from your glorious dwellings and loved the lowliness of our humanity; You dwelt in the womb of the Blessed Virgin who was sanctified, body and soul, through the gifts of the Holy Spirit.

> She is the one who was exalted above all creation, because the Word of life took flesh from her.

> She is the one of whom our mouths are incapable of praising, because she became the Mother of God the Word.

> She is the one from whose sanctified womb appeared the hope of life and the salvation of mankind.

> She is the one who became the generous stream, because she gave the water of new life to quench the thirst of the world.

> She is the one who received the Heavenly Bread who nourished all nations; she is the one in whom dwelt the heavenly promise Who dissipated anguish from the hearts of all people.

> She is the one who became the holy of holies, the dwelling place of her High Priest and the acceptable incense.

She is the one after whom the symbols of the saintly prophets have been modeled.

All foretold events have been accomplished through you! O Blessed Virgin Mary: you are the beatitude of the Prophets, the joy of the Apostles, the crown of the Martyrs, the strength of the Confessors, the pride of the heavenly hosts, the aide of the sick and suffering and the consolation of the poor and sorrowful.

We now implore you O Blessed Virgin, Mother of God the Word, to intercede for us to Christ who dawned from you to grant us, on this day of your memorial, the forgiveness of our sins. May He also grant harmony to the Churches, peace to the Monasteries, purity to the priests, understanding to the shepherds, healing to the sick, comfort to the depressed, consolation to the sorrowful, satisfaction to the needy, return to those who are far away, guidance to the stranded, freedom to the imprisoned, salvation to the exiled, happiness to the troubled, hope to the distressed! And to those who have asked and will ask for our prayers, may the Lord send them an angel of peace and mercy to deliver them, on this day of your memorial, O pure and Blessed Virgin. May He give rest to the bodies and souls of our parents, brothers and teachers who have died in the true faith; with them, we shall offer Him glory, now and forever.

People: Amen.

7. The Saturday Prayer

Proemion

May we offer praise, glory and honor to the Most High who chose the lowly daughter to honor Him; to the Exalted One who looked at the humility of his maiden and made her a paradise for his glory; to the Lord Who glorified the memory of His Mother in heaven and on earth and honored her feast day in the Church, His bride; the Good One to whom are due glory and honor, now and forever.

People: Amen.

Sedro

We petition you O Blessed Virgin, Mother of the Only Son; the Holy Mountain upon which the Divine fire was ignited; the bush which was not consumed by the burning fire; the fortified tower in which the King of glory prayed; the meek dove who enchanted the Eagle— the ancient of days; the blessed vine who carried the precious grape who has sweetened all of mankind; the new salt whose taste has rectified the entire creation; the lighted lamp whose light shines in the wilderness! O Glory of the Church and pride of the world, O paradise of lights who is adorned with the divine rays: you are the new shoot who replaced the old grapevine because you gave us the Life that renews our old nature!

And now, O Blessed Virgin Mary, petition your Son Who took flesh from you and divinized us, Who humbled himself and exalted us, Who impoverished himself and enriched us, that He may adorn us with virtues, and imprint in our hearts lofty aspirations leading to heaven. May He strengthen our intellect with meditation and spiritual knowledge so that we may attain the heavenly realms. May He lead us to divine perfection so that, in jubilation, we may continually celebrate your glorious feast day, honor your blessed memorial and be made worthy of your prayers. Then, we shall offer glory to the One Who appeared from you, to His Father and His Holy Spirit, now and forever.

People: Amen.

8. The Annunciation Prayer

Proemion

May we offer praise, glory and honor to the Son Who has neither beginning nor end; Who, by the will of His Father, the action of the Holy Spirit and the announcement of Gabriel, dwelt in the Virgin Mary for our salvation. He dawned into the world as a man without any change in His nature; the Good One to whom are due glory and honor this morning and all the days of our lives, now and forever.

People: Amen.

Sedro

Glory, praise and adoration to the Father, the Son and the Holy Spirit: to the Father Who sent his only Son to save Adam and bring him back to the paradise he had lost through his own fault; to the Son who descended to earth and took flesh from the pure Virgin; to the Holy Spirit who overshadowed Mary to give birth to the savior of mankind.

Blessed are you Mary, because all generations honor you. All people of the earth praise the One who has chosen you for his Mother. Blessed are you, because Gabriel visited Nazareth on this day. Blessed are you, because in you dwelt the One who created the world and established the foundations of the universe. Blessed are you, because through you, Adam could now raise his head after he was humiliated by the serpent in paradise. Blessed are you, because you are the glory of all nations and the pride of all generations.

We now implore you, O Word of God, as we petition you through the prayers of your Virgin Mother: keep away from your Church every division and conflict; establish your peace throughout the world; strengthen your churches, protect your monasteries; purify your priests; let justice and charity reign among people. Through your cross watch over your servants, men and women and protect the virgins. Unite into your kingdom all those who are gathered today to honor the memorial of your Blessed Mother. When you come to judge all peoples of the earth, do not judge us according to the failures we have committed, but be our hope, for we have no hope except in you and acknowledge us before your Father for we have acknowledged you in the world. Grant rest to those who have departed from us, so that they may praise you in your kingdom. Accept the incense which we have now offered. Then, we shall raise hymns of praise and thanksgiving to You, to Your Father and to Your Holy Spirit, now and forever.

People: Amen.

9. The Visitation Prayer

Proemion

May we offer praise, glory and honor to the true God Who could neither be fathomed by the human mind nor be seen by the naked eye; to Whom alone belong perfect knowledge and total comprehension; Who has created all things seen and unseen; Who has neither beginning nor end and Who is adored and praised through His two natures and two wills; the Good One to whom are due glory and honor, this morning and all the days of our lives, now and forever.

People: Amen.

Sedro

O Lord, who dwell in the heights, you are served by the seraphim and glorified by the cherubim, you have descended from your heavens and came to us. You have entered the house of Zechariah and poured out your mercy upon your forerunner. Today, the words of the prophet are fulfilled: "Rejoice, O Mount Zion, and leap with joy, O daughters of Judea." Today, the barren rejoices saying: "come in peace O burning bush of Moses, fleece of Gideon, lamp of the sanctuaries of Zechariah." "Come in peace O full of grace, you are blessed among women and blessed is the fruit of your womb."

May we, poor sinners, sing with Elizabeth saying: Hail Mary the Blessed Virgin, through you, our sins are forgiven and from you we have received the Word of life. Hail Mary, through you, we were raised from our fall and we have returned from our ignorance, our darkness has dissipated and our strength was restored.

Therefore, we commemorate this happy feast with spiritual hymns, asking you, O Word of God, through our prayers and incense, grant us your grace, enlighten us with your light, confirm us in the true faith, so that our joy may bring us to you and may we desire, with all our hearts, to meet you. Then, we the living, along with our faithful departed, shall give glory to You, to your Father and to your Holy Spirit, now and forever.

People: Amen.

10. The Assumption Prayer

Proemion

May we offer praise glory and honor to the hidden Father who has sent his Son to be born of the Blessed Virgin Mary; to the Sun of justice, Who has dawned from her through his grace and enlightened the whole universe; to the Holy Spirit who made her a dwelling place for himself—a marvelous bride without blemish or sin; the Good One to whom are due glory and honor now, at all times, and forever.

People: Amen.

Sedro

O Blessed Virgin Mary, on this day we complete your memorial and celebrate the feast of your Assumption into heaven, body and soul, you who are full of grace and abundant in mercy. You have become a second heaven and carried the Lord of all creation. Heaven and earth and all creation glorifies the feast of your Assumption saying: Blessed are you, because the gates of heaven are open before you and the seraphim welcome you in glory! The Apostles have gathered around you from all corners of the earth! Peter came from Rome, John from Ephesus, Thomas from India, Andrew from Persia, James from Jerusalem, the son of Alphaeus from Serug, Thaddaeus from Edessa, Bartholomew from Armenia, Simon of Cyrene from Cyprus and Judas, son of James, from Seleucia-Ctesiphon. They were all ready for this day of the Assumption of the Blessed Virgin who is full of grace; they all chanted for her, the hymn of the Holy Spirit, with beautiful voices singing: come in peace, O ship carrying the Life of the world. Come in peace, O Mother of Jesus, our Lord and our God. Come in peace, you whom the Fathers, the Prophets and the Saints yearn to see. Come in peace, O holy and Blessed Mother, the pride of humanity, the purest among women, and the glory of the universe.

Today, O Blessed Virgin Mary we petition you on the feast of your Assumption: beseech your only Son to grant us peaceful and joyful times, to remove anger and afflictions from the world. May He sustain the elderly and instruct the children. May He grant wisdom to the young, safeguard the orphans, satisfy the needy, assist the priests and save the exiled.

May He grant us all the forgiveness of sins and failings, give rest to the faithful who have departed from us and receive them into the heavenly paradise where we all are invited to meet you. Then, together, we shall offer praise to the glorious Trinity, the Father, the Son and the Holy Spirit, forever and ever.

People: Amen.

11. A Hymn from the Sunday Morning Prayer

This is the third strophe chosen from the hymn of the three boys and composed after the third *"Fsheeto"* tune.

> The entire land of Ephesus was showered with dew when Saint John revealed an apparition about the Blessed Virgin Mary. In it is written that there should be three memorials a year for the Blessed Virgin Mary: Let January be the feast of planting of the seeds, May the feast of harvest and August the feast of grapes, because in these months, the mysteries of life are prefigured.

12. *Sooghyoto* of the Virgin

> A. Who can comprehend the treasury of your goodness, O Blessed Mother of God!
> Simon the Zealot, the servant of God, learned from you the greatest of righteousness.

> B. Simeon the Stylite, the venerable, and Alexius preached of your love;
> Saint Zephyrinus, the Lebanese, trained your admirers to adopt your virtues.

C. Nicholas, the victorious, destroyed all types of idolatries;
    Through your intercession, he scattered the wolves and
    crushed the heresies of the treacherous Arius.

D. You have sustained all Martyrs including Saint Stephen:
    Proto-Martyr and head of Deacons;
    Saints George and Theodorus, through your power, have
    defeated the villains.

E. Saint Anthony, the Father of monks along with the first
    hermits, they have modeled their lives after yours;
    Saint Maron suckled from your purity and nourished the
    inhabitants of Lebanon.

F. Saint Macarius, the Abbot, and Arsanius dedicated their
    lives to sing your praises;
    Saint Gregory drew from the treasury of your virtues and
    distributed them to all nations.

G. Saint Basil, through your intercession, humiliated the
    heretics;
    Saint Athanasius, in his teachings, roared like a lion
    against your adversaries.

H. Saint Cyril silenced all those who proclaimed the one
    nature;
    Saint John Chrysostom enriched the Church after having
    been endowed by your abundant treasures.

I. Saint Ephrem, through your virtues, has nourished the
    multitude of Hermits;
    Saints Ignatius and Arthemius had shone like the sun
    among those who struggled.

J. Saint Dionysius, through your guidance, has shone among
    the heavenly powers;
    O you who surpasses all praise, intercede for us, we your
    poor and lowly servants.

K. Keep away all kinds of divisions from every community and eliminate from us all worldly temptations;
Straighten our paths in justice and spare us from the snares of the evil one.

L. We sing praise to you, every morning and sunrise, O most compassionate Mother;
and constantly proclaim with one voice: may your prayers be with us, O glory of the ends of the earth.

M. We glorify God, the Father, the Only Son, and the Holy Spirit with voices of praise;
For his mercy, in glorious songs, during this life and in the life to come.

CHAPTER VIII

Mary in the Maronite
Qurbono or Mass

The *Qurbono* is the Passover of the Lord. It is the supper-meeting with the risen Jesus. The Eucharist is the constant thanksgiving prayer offered to God because of His love for humanity which He accomplished through his plan of salvation. In the *Qurbono* the Church lives the entire divine plan, which is the Incarnation, the Death, the Resurrection and Pentecost.

The Maronite *Qurbono* is the true Offering of the Community in which she is fully present through the prayers, the chanting, the readings, the offerings and the life-giving Holy Spirit. One of the main characteristics of the Maronite *Qurbono* is the fact that it is quite "popular" and close to the community by preserving the actual and lively participation of the people.

Is it conceivable that the Virgin Mary may be absent from the Maronite *Qurbono*? Would she be out of this continuous divine plan and would it be possible that she is absent from its supplications, hymns, petitions and chanting? Going back in detail to each and every part of the *Qurbono*, we find that the Virgin Mary is present in it from the beginning until the end, as if she is in Cana saying to the faithful before the water is changed into wine: "Do whatever He tells you."

As we present the Maronite *Qurbono*, we shall encounter the Virgin Mary at each and every liturgical juncture accompanying the faithful step by step until they leave the church.

The Maronite *Qurbono* is divided into three parts:

1. The first is preparatory and runs from the beginning until the end of the *Hoosoyo*

2. The second is educational and consists of the Readings and the homily

3. The third is Eucharistic and includes the presentation of the offerings, their consecration and the partaking of the Body and Blood of Christ, i.e., Communion.

The Virgin Mary is present in all three of them.

Part One: The Preparatory

The Deacon lights the candles and the priest prepares the bread and wine then the congregation begins: "Praise the Lord all you nations, Alleluia," chanting to Christ, to the Virgin Mary, to the martyrs and to the dead. The dedicated verse to the Virgin Mary translates as follows:

> May the prayer of the Blessed Virgin be for our protection, Alleluia:
>
> Mary, the Lord has chosen you among all people, because He found you to be the purest and holiest of all creatures;
> He dwelt in your womb for nine months and from your body He took flesh.

This weak Arabic translation is relatively recent and may date back to the sixteenth century. The original text is in Aramaic and dates to a period preceding the tenth century. It summarizes for us that the Virgin Mary is the Mother of God; she is the one that the Lord has chosen from among all women of the world.

The following prayers, which constitute the proper of the day or the feast, and the *Hoosoyo* which consists of the rite of forgiveness, are a collection that could be entirely dedicated to the feasts of the Virgin

Mary. As for other feasts, the popular devotion has preserved the following hymn:

> O purest of all people, may your prayers be with us,
> we pray that you may constantly sustain us;
> beseech the Lord, your Son, so that He may have mercy on us
> through your prayers.

This is only one verse from a common collection of both petitions and commemorations recited by the people while the priest silently remembers the Lord Jesus and His plan of salvation and the intentions for which the *Qurbono* is offered. In the beginning of this collection there is a mention of the Lord Jesus and His plan of salvation. In this plan of salvation, the priest mentions all those who pleased the Lord from Adam to the present and "especially the blessed and glorified Ever-virgin Mary, Mother of God..." In special Marian memorials, the priest prays silently asking the Virgin Mary that his prayers be accepted and his sins forgiven.

However, in the special Marian devotion, there are prayers of forgiveness known as *"Sedre"* composed in both prose and poetry and dedicated to Mary, the most common of which is mentioned in the daily *Qurbono*:

A. The Prose *Sedre*
"As we praise and glorify with spiritual hymns, the Blessed Ever-virgin Mary, Mother of God, we ask her to petition the fruit of her womb, for us saying: O Lord, through the prayers of your Mother, keep away from the earth and all its inhabitants the scourge of wrath..."[18]

B. The Poetry *Sedre*
Hail Mary, you are the Mother of the all-powerful God;
Who filled heaven and earth with His power and might...!

These two *Sedre* are found in the *Qurbono* Book with their Aramaic and Arabic texts dating back to the period preceding the tenth century. The main theme in both of them reflects the intercession of Mary to God because she has influence with her Son.

---

[18] This *Sedro* is published earlier in the Sunday prayer, (p. 82).

The majority of priests, in recent practice, used the *Sedro* of the Virgin Mary instead of the *Sedro* that is dedicated for the particular day or feast. According to some old Maronite manuscripts, this may have been an old custom dating back, at least, to more than six hundred years.

Part Two: The Readings and the Homily

The Readings are specifically dedicated to each feast and memorial and prefaced by a hymn known as the psalm of praise. It is actually the psalm of the Readings dedicated to Marian feasts and memorials as well as to the Wednesday prayer. This is a special hymn for Mary and is chanted either in Aramaic or in Arabic:

> Blessed are you O Holy Mother, you are glorified for your virginity, because from you appeared in holiness, the blessed fruit of the Father;

> It is proper to honor the memorial of the Holy Virgin Mary, because she carried the One who carries all creation.

In this simple hymn, there is a deep Marian theological echo which is an explanation to what has been recorded in the Gospel about the blessedness of the one who is full of grace.

The above mentioned hymn is the psalm of the Readings which takes place before the Epistle. However, before the Gospel, during the feasts of the Virgin Mary, the Alleluia response is a verse chosen from the Psalter, which is accompanied by the "Alleluia" chant. It reads as follows: "Alleluia, Alleluia, the King's daughter stands in glory, and the queen stands at your right hand, Alleluia." This, of course, points at the Virgin Mary as the daughter of David, the queen who is standing at the right hand side of her Son in Paradise.

Part Three: The Eucharist or the Offering of the Gifts

This part begins by transferring the gifts to the main altar. Prior to the procession, a diaconal proclamation known as *"Korozooto"* and consisting of three verses, is chanted in Aramaic during Marian feasts and memorials, and translated as follows:

> Blessed are you Mary, daughter of David, because the heavenly Father was pleased in you becoming the mother of His only Son through whom all nations will be blessed.
>
> Blessed are you Mary, daughter of David, because the Holy Spirit dwelt in you and made you a beautiful temple in which the Lord of the heights will abide.
>
> Blessed are you Mary, daughter of David, because you carried in your arms He who carries heaven and earth and whose power is beyond description.

These three simple verses show the connection of the Virgin Mary to the Holy Trinity. The Virgin Mary does not appear alone before the Church, but she is in a constant relation with the triune God. She is the daughter of David in whom the Father was pleased so He has chosen her, the Holy Spirit has sanctified her and the Son dwelt within her womb. Mary is also remembered along with the gifts that are offered upon the altar. She is present in the Church and with the Church, because she is the symbol of the Church, the mystical Body of Christ. When the priests process the gifts over the altar... "the Church sings" to Christ, the Bread of Life whom the Father sent to the world as a grain of wheat in rich soil... then the Church remembers Mary, the Mother of Life, and chants in Aramaic the following hymn:

> ... Alleluia:
> O Mother of the Life, petition your divine Son to keep away from us all misfortune, to ward off from among us all conflicts and to guide us on the right path. On this day of your memorial, we give praise to your only Son, our Savior.
> Alleluia, accept our prayers.

At the exchange of the kiss of peace, just before proceeding to the Eucharistic Prayer, the deacon announces a second proclamation which is called the "middle one" the commemorations of the Church over the gifts and begins with the following:

"Mary, the pride of Virgins, we remember her through these Offerings..."

In the Eucharistic prayer, according to the old Maronite *Anaphora* of *"Sharrar,"* Mary is remembered after the commemoration of Christ and before the invocation of the Holy Spirit:

Celebrant:
We remember, especially, the Glorious, Blessed, Ever-virgin Mary, Mother of God.

Deacon:
"Remember her, O Lord, and through her pure and acceptable prayers, have mercy on us, forgive us and answer us."

Celebrant:
(Silently before the invocation of the Holy Spirit): "O Mother of our Lord Jesus, petition your only Son to forgive my sins and to accept from my poor and sinful hands, the sacrifice which I have offered through your intercessions, O holy and Blessed Mother."

This was according to the Eastern Syriac *Anaphora* of *Sharrar* which is common between the Maronites and the Chaldeans. But according to the other Western Syriac Maronite *Anaphora*s there is another petition specified for the Virgin Mary and for all the Saints.

At the breaking of the Bread, the deacon announces the third proclamation which begins with the expression "Let us all petition with humility..." in it there is a special petition to the Virgin Mary:

O Blessed Virgin Mary, our Lady and our Mother, beseech your only Son to be pleased with our prayers and to have mercy on us.

On Marian feasts, the entire proclamation is dedicated to the Virgin Mary. For example in the Wednesday service it reads:

Come forth O faithful and receive the abundant graces during the memorial of the Virgin Mary, and through it receive the mysteries in faith and warm love.

Finally, at the conclusion of the *Qurbono*, and before the final blessing, the people sing a hymn dedicated for the memorial of the Virgin Mary one verse of which reads as follows:

> "Alleluia, O Mother of God, the descending and ascending ladder of Jacob was modeled after you, because the Son of God, who is the hope of the bereaved, descended to the world through you, and saved us from the evil one."

Most often this verse is chanted all by itself during the feasts and the memorials of the Virgin Mary, "Of Blessed Memory," just as people proclaim whenever they mention her name.

As it has been mentioned earlier, the commemoration of the Virgin Mary in the *Qurbono* accompanies all actions and prayers, as if she is one of the faithful who attends and participates in the new wedding banquet of Cana.

Al-Ephremiat:[19]

The Ephremiat is a popular poem composed of seven strophes and modeled after the Syriac tune known as the tune of (Mar Ephram) or "Saint Ephrem," thus the term "Ephremiat." Although there are some "Ephremiat" composed of twelve strophes, they are modeled after the Syriac tune known as the tune of (Mar Yacoub) or "Saint Jacob," thus the term "Ya'coubiat." These Syriac poetic hymns were translated into Lebanese poetry under the title of "Qirrady" or classic Lebanese songs; they are Ephremiat in style but "Ya'coubiat" in meaning and content.

The Ephremiat is a poem which describes the nature of the feast and is sung during the *Qurbono*. In the Maronite Ephremiat book, there is a collection of nine poems for the various Marian feasts. The most ancient and meaningful one is "We offer you peace..." this is the only one found in Aramaic, the rest are in Arabic, most of which are composed since the eighteenth century. "We offer you peace ..." and "Hail Mary..." in Aramaic are composed according to the Ya'coubiat

---

[19] Refer to the book of Boutros Gemayel on *Maronite Qurbono*, Beirut 1970, (pp. 141-143).

tune and found in the old manuscripts of the Maronite *Qurbono* the most famous of which are: manuscript 619 of Aleppo from the year 1490 and the Syriac manuscript 29 of the Vatican, written in Cyprus, from the year 1535. As far as we know, this hymn is not known among the Jacobite manuscripts. It was originally published in Syriac in all of the printed *Qurbono* books. It was translated into Arabic in this present condition in the eighteenth century.

This type of hymn is educational and follows the most favorable and popular method. In spite of its weak Arabic language, most of its leading themes still clearly reflect the following:

- The Virgin Mary was "chosen before the Sun":
     Mary is present in God's plan of salvation.
- With her milk, she nourished the One who feeds all creation:
     Mary is the Mother of God.
- All generations will call her blessed.
- We ask that she intercedes with her Son for us.

Once these popular hymns are properly translated into a simple language and rid of errors, we hope that we could make use of them and chant them.

The following is the text of the Ephremiat for the Virgin Mary:

We offer you peace, O Mother of the all-powerful God, the Most High, who filled heaven and earth of His power and might;
We offer you peace, because, before the Sun was created, you became the mother of the chosen One and remained the pride of virgins.

We offer you peace, O Mother of the Son and daughter of the Father—the ancient of Days—who, created Adam from nothing;
We offer you peace, because you gave birth to the Lord of Lords who made Adam and Eve give thanks to the most generous giver.

Blessed are you, Mary, you became the Mother of the Most Holy, who granted holiness of souls to the sons of Levi;
Blessed are you, Mary, because in all purity, the shining light of the Father, the Son of the eternal God, dwelt in your womb.

Rejoice O Mary, because from your breasts you nourished the Creator who feeds all creation;
Rejoice, because you carried in your arms, with extraordinary love, the One who is attended by the powers on High.

All generations of the earth give praise to the Blessed Virgin Mary, because He who was born from her erased the bill of debts;
And we, her poor servants, offer to her our deepest supplications saying: intercede for us, you who answer every repentant sinner.

Beseech the One, who through your purity, has shone like a morning star, to have mercy on our community who gathered to honor your memory;
Through your intercession, may He accept from us, the sacrifice we have offered and be pleased with it for the rest of our lives and on the day of Judgment.

We glorify You, O Lord, who dawned from Mary and dissipated all darkness, you who appeared in two natures and in two wills, only Son of the Father;
We give thanks to You, to your Father and to your Holy Spirit, three persons, One God, without division.

We offer praise to the Father, to the Son and to the Holy Spirit so that we may be granted mercy in the new and everlasting life.

CHAPTER IX

Mary in the Maronite Procession or (Ziyah)

Recently, we have been accustomed to give the title "Procession" to the paraliturgical service of the benediction. In this devotion, with which our churches honor the icon of the Virgin Mary, we pray and chant the hymns "O Mother of God..., and Although your body..." Then the priest imparts the blessing with the Icon. Thus, this devotion began to be called (Ziyah Al-Adra) or "Procession of the Virgin Mary." Is this the actual Procession?

1. The Procession (Ziyah)

The Arabic word "al-ziyah" derives from *Zouyoho* in Aramaic, which means "to move from one particular place to another designated one." In the colloquial language, when we ask someone to "move..." we mean for that person to walk or travel. In a liturgical sense, however, this move does not mean just a simple walk or travel, but an organized communal walk within a specified religious procession.

Such processions have been known as "parades, rounds, marches or organized walks."

What are the reasons for these organized religious processions?

Before the Christian era, processions and organized ceremonies have played a significant role in the Jewish and the Pagan religions, as well as in the ancient Egyptian, Babylonian, Phoenician and many other religions.

During the main holidays, the crowds would gather around the temple. The priests would carry the statue of the worshiped god and process it among the people, taking it out into the streets of the city, while they are singing and praying. In the Christian era, the oldest of these popular religious appearances is the festival in which the people received Christ into Jerusalem on the "day of the palms" when they carried palm branches and came out to meet him shouting "Hosanna to the King." He mounted a donkey and accepted to enter Jerusalem amid acclaims and loud voices as if the "day of the Kingdom" has begun. The "Palm Sunday Procession" is the beginning of all Christian processions and still is, until today, the greatest Maronite procession.

Therefore, the procession takes the nature of an organized popular religious walking ceremony, commemorating a religious event or repeating the same event, characterized in exhilaration and joy. In such processions, jubilation and shouts of joy are mixed with people's prayers and petitions asking for God's blessings.

Another important procession in our Maronite rituals is that of the Cross. [20]

By the "Procession of the Cross" we do not refer to the ceremony of the blessing with the Cross on the Fridays of Lent; this is not the procession of the Cross! The current liturgical books do not call it as such. The 1909 Edition of the *Book of Rituals* calls it the "Benediction with the Holy Cross commemorating the burial of the Savior." This same book provides the title "Procession of the Cross" to the ceremony that takes place on the Sunday of the Resurrection. This ceremony is also celebrated on the feast of the Exaltation of the Glorious Cross on September 14.

The Maronite ceremony of the "Procession of the Cross" was published, for the first time, in Rome in 1647 under the title "the Procession of the Cross for the Sunday of the Resurrection" adopted from the 1581 Syriac manuscript number 403, which is preserved in the Vatican.

---

[20] Reverend Boutros Gemayel, Liturgical Ceremonies for Great Friday of the Crucifixion and the Resurrection. *The Clergy Periodical*, 11, 1961, (pp. 249-266).

There is only one ceremony for the procession of the Cross in the old Maronite manuscripts. It is the archetype of all ceremonies and takes place on Resurrection Sunday. What does this procession consist of? It is summarized in the following liturgical characteristics:

A. On Resurrection Sunday, the faithful enter the Church before the high Mass. They go to the tomb as they chant "Christ is risen from the dead." They carry the Cross and process it throughout the church, then outside the church, and perhaps they take it out, in a larger procession, into the streets of the town accompanied by incense, candles and flowers along with music, songs and joyful shouts repeating: "Christ is risen from the dead..."

B. At the conclusion of the procession, from the highest point of the sanctuary, the priest blesses the four corners of the universe with the Cross as he recites the "blessing" or the "litany of the feast" while the people ask for the "blessing" in light of the triumph of Christ and His Resurrection which is expressed through this religious "festivity."

It is after this archetypical old procession that the Church modeled other paraliturgical devotions such as the "Benediction of the Icon of the Virgin Mary," the Benediction of the Icon of Saint Maron and that of many other saints. Thus, the procession consists of people carrying the icon in the church, then outside the church, and possibly taking it out into the streets of the town.

This type of procession in honor of the Blessed Mother was basically celebrated a few times a year at her major feast days such as the "Praises of the Mother of God," the "Assumption" which falls on August 15 and the "Annunciation." With time, Western influence added more processions to the original Maronite procession such as:

• The Procession of the Blessed Sacrament on the feast of Corpus Christi;

• The Procession of the icon of Our Lady of the Holy Rosary on the first Sunday of October;

- The Procession of the icon of the Scapular of Our Lady of Mount Carmel on July 16.

The title "Procession" was mistakenly given to every small ceremony consisting of a blessing with a certain icon. Therefore, throughout our explanation of the present liturgical ceremonies we will differentiate between Procession and Benediction. In the 1909 Edition of the *Book of Rituals*, which is currently in use, we clearly differentiate between the two as we find the following:

- The Procession of the Holy Cross on Resurrection Sunday and on the Exaltation of the Glorious Cross

- The Benediction with the Holy Cross on the Fridays of Lent

- The Procession of the Blessed Sacrament on the feast of Corpus Christi

- The Benediction with the Blessed Sacrament every Sunday evening

- The Procession of the Icon of Our Lady of the Rosary on the first Sunday of October

- The Benediction with the Icon of the Virgin Mary

- The Procession of the Icon of Saint Maron on the feast of Saint Maron

- The Benediction with the Icon of Saint Maron every second Sunday of the month.

Add to these the "procession which takes place at baptism," at the ceremony of Crowning and at the sacerdotal ordinations... Each of these processions has its own detailed meanings, but in general, at the conclusion of the sacramental ceremony, the procession encircles the Church once or three times, in order to achieve a designated liturgical purpose. At baptism, the procession means an "organized walk" from the baptismal font, where baptism took place, to the church, where the "baptized" enters to participate in the Eucharist. The procession involves candles, incense and singing of hymns. As for the newly wed, at the ceremony of crowning, the bride, the groom and their witnesses will be crowned with flowers. The crowned bride and groom will process among the people. The procession could go as far as the house of the groom as he takes "his bride" into his home amid shouts of joy and festivities.

The procession of sacerdotal ordinations is the candidate's initial step whereby he practices his function among the people right after his ordination. If he was ordained a lector, he would carry the Lectionary Book and processes it among the people; if he was ordained a priest, he would carry the Holy Eucharist among the people so as to offer it to them thereafter at Communion...!

In conclusion, we must first differentiate between the two situations. Then we must go back to the roots and live the liturgy in all of its significant meanings. We must separate the Procession, which takes place during the celebration of a holy day, from the Benediction with the icon, which takes place during common memorials.

The Procession consists of all people participating in an organized liturgical ceremony: the clergy and the entire congregation along with candles, incense, flowers, and musical instruments such as cymbals, triangles and fans... Obviously, this is celebrated during a "Holy Day" and at major Marian feasts.

As for the Benediction with the icon, it has its own nature wherein the priest carries the icon facing the people and then blesses them with it at the conclusion of the devotional service.

2. The Revival of Marian Processions

We recommend that the Procession of the icon of the Virgin Mary, whether in the Church or outside, adopt the following format:

> A. In major celebrations and feast days, the icon may be carried from the church while the procession is being organized to venerate the Virgin Mary in an orderly fashion. The entire congregation is to participate,

especially in the singing, coupled with exhilaration, shouts of joy, ringing bells, clanging cymbals, waving fans along with banners, lighted candles and the burning of perfumed smoked incense.

B. The singing of the litany then takes place whereby the cantor leads with the verse while people respond with the refrain. During the procession, there might be some stations where the priest blesses the people with the icon as they sing appropriate hymns. Throughout history, Church leaders had commanded that processions must be celebrated not only on feast days but also when disasters struck such as wars, plagues, droughts and locust invasion... The people, going out to the streets carrying crosses and icons, called upon God as they shared their trials and misfortunes in a more direct and concrete way.

The purpose of these celebrations is to rekindle the torch of faith in the heart of the "faithful." But if and when that fire is ever extinguished, there would be no need for "Processions" because they may easily become empty appearances subject to mockery and slander.

Before we conclude our talk about the "Procession of the Virgin Mary," we ought to mention a word about the integration of the Rosary into our homes and churches. After giving a brief history on the integration of the Rosary, we shall provide the text of the two Maronite litanies along with the hymns with the Benediction of the icon and a short history for each of them.

3. The Rosary and the Maronites

The Rosary, these blessed olive beads which trickle between our fingers, is not of recent history. It originated in the East and may have begun in India. It became popular among Moslems with the term "*masbahat*" in Arabic, which means "to give praise." Devout Moslems used it in repeating attributes of God with its beads, just as it was used by Christian hermits. It reached the West through European monks after the Crusades! The monks who contributed the most to spread its devotion are the brothers of Abed El-Ahad, Dominic, known as the Dominicans.

The Rosary was a popular method of prayers, which has spread in the West during the Middle Ages; it is, in fact, a simple and easy prayer for all individuals, families and communities. Since then, Popes have continually encouraged the faithful to pray the Rosary. The most famous Pope who organized the Rosary was Pope Paul V in his 1569 encyclical. More Popes later, in their apostolic letters, renewed their encouragements to pray the Rosary. The most recent one appeared after the Second Vatican Council, the apostolic exhortation of Pope Paul VI, entitled the "Devotion to the Virgin Mary," which was published on February 2, 1974. The exhortation talked at length about the Rosary and urged people to pray the family Rosary. We conclude from the papal exhortation the following directives:

The Rosary of the Virgin Mary consists of the following:

a. The meditation with Mary, on the series of the mysteries of salvation, is distributed into three parts expressing the Joy of the Coming of Jesus, the Sorrow of his saving Passion and the Glory of his Resurrection;

b. The Our Father, which is the base of the Christian prayer;

c. The greeting of the Angel and Elizabeth, and the supplication of the Church praying: Hail Mary full of grace... Holy Mary Mother of God...;

The repetition of this greeting is a special characteristic of the Rosary. The number of greetings is one hundred fifty which, in fact, resembles the Psalter that contains one hundred fifty psalms. With time, the Rosary was divided into five decades;

d. The prayer concludes by giving "Glory to the Father and to the Son and to the Holy Spirit!"

Pope Paul VI says:

"We would like now to join our voice to the voices of our predecessors and strongly recommend the prayer of the

Rosary in the family… because the Christian family is thus a family church…! Therefore, her children may together raise their prayers to God. If the family neglected this communal prayer, it would lose its character as a Christian family…"

"In addition to the prayer of the Divine Office, which is the highest point the family prayer can attain, there, the Rosary of the Virgin Mary would be, the most preferable communal prayer for the Christian family."

The Pope concludes his recommendations saying:

"We would like to repeat that the Rosary is an excellent and magnificent prayer; those who work to spread its devotion should be careful not to exceed its defined boundaries."

The Rosary cannot be considered foreign to our Church today. The Maronites have emphasized the prayer of the Rosary more than four hundred years ago. Father Eliano, a Jesuit monk, mentioned that during his visit to the Maronites in the year 1580, he brought them "around one thousand rosaries."

In his most recent pastoral letter on September 8, 1987, on the occasion of the Marian Year, His Beatitude Patriarch Nasrallah Peter Sfeir called upon the Maronite people to honor the Mother of God by praying the Rosary.

If the Rosary was a common method of prayer in the East among Christians and non-Christians, and even if it came to us through Western missionaries, it was, and still is, an easy but rich method of prayer helping the faithful to meditate upon the mysteries of God, along with his companion—the Mother of God and our Mother—on the journey of salvation. In praying the Rosary we find, particularly in the family, an excellent method to bring its members together in the faith under the protection of the one who intercedes for Christians who, throughout their lives, have never spared lavishing upon her the most honorable titles.

On October 16, 2002 the late Pope John Paul II issued an apostolic letter entitled the "Rosary of the Virgin Mary." He announced that the "Year of the Rosary" extends from October 2002 until October

2003. He added to the actual "Rosary" the five Luminous Mysteries, which would follow the Joyful Mysteries, based on the public life of Jesus and its basic stations. The Luminous Mysteries begin with the Baptism of Jesus. They take us from the Baptism at the Jordan River to Jesus attending the wedding at Cana, passing through Conversion and the Proclamation of the Kingdom, and finally arriving at the Transfiguration and the Last Supper. Thus, leading us to the Sorrowful Mysteries and concluding with the Glorious Mysteries.

4. Litanies and Hymns

A. We Worship You, O Lord Our Savior

This "Litany" is actually a hymn which accompanies the Benediction of the icon of the Virgin Mary. It is considered a litany due to the successive recurrence of the words "we petition you..." It is translated from a Syriac tune known "the minor," which is commonly used for processions such as the tune of the Palm Sunday Procession (come forth O dear brethren) and many other hymns...!

This Litany is divided into two parts; the first is giving praise to the Virgin Mary; and the second is a series of petitions.

There is a clear theological depth in giving praise to Mary. It is a prayer of thanksgiving to God for giving Mary to us who truly is the Daughter of the Father, the Mother of the Son and the Spouse of the Holy Spirit.

Through Mary, prophesies were fulfilled according to the divine plan. This part concludes with two verses one depicts Mary filled with the divine light, the second mentions that through her, the mysteries were completed and Adam was spared.

As for the second part, throughout the petitions, Mary is seen as the one whom God has chosen to intercede for us with her Son. She is a clear image reflecting the needs of the people, i.e., purity of heart, health for the body, the daily bread, healing for the sick and rest for the dead. The concluding verse serves as a greeting to the "most honorable and gracious" Virgin Mary.

This Litany is purely Syriac in nature, Maronite in tradition, sweet in expression and simple in tune. That is why all its meanings come out when it is chanted between two groups of people along with the sound of cymbals and triangles during the procession of the Icon of the Virgin Mary, be it in the Church or outside.

The text of the Litany is as follows:

We worship you O our Savior for you have graced us
with the pure Virgin Mary who, at all times, intercedes for us.
Blessed are you, O daughter of the Father and Mother of the Son who protects us.
O Spouse of the Holy Spirit, to you we raise our supplications.
The prophets foretold about you as David, your grandfather, prophesied
that from you, Jesus will be born, the Son of God who will save us.
You are the fleece of Gideon bring to us the heavenly dew.
You are the weapon of the all-powerful God through whom we defeat our enemies.
Daniel has envisioned you as a high and fortified mountain.
The Lord has overshadowed you and has filled you with divine light.
In you all Mysteries were completed and Adam, our father, was spared.
O Mary we petition you, deliver us from the evil one.
O Mary we petition you, protect us from falling into sin.
O Mary we petition you, save us from the plague.
O Mary we petition you, grant us the heavenly graces.
O Mary we petition you, bless the fruits of our land.
O Mary we petition you, heal the ailing sick.
O Mary we petition you, assist the faithful departed.
May the peace of God remain always with you O Mother of Jesus our Savior.

B. Mary Intercede for Your Servants

This Litany belongs to the type of Alphabetical Syriac hymns, which means that the first verse starts with the letter A, the second follows with the letter B, the third with C and so forth... It is composed according to the Syriac tune known as *Ho Qteelo Bmesren*... In fact, it is modeled after the tune of *Ya Sha'bee Wa Sahbee,* O my People O my Friends, and that of *Ana Al Umul Hazeena,* I am the Sorrowful Mother, which is one of the more common Syriac tunes. The content of the Litany consists of praises whereby each verse reveals a beautiful spiritual image of the Virgin Mary. Unlike the previous litany, here we do not find recurrent "petitions" from the faithful asking for personal needs. But rather a series of verses through which the faithful honor the Virgin Mary with various titles such as the Mother of the Merciful God, Pure Virgin, Temple of God, Paradise of Life, High Mountain and Morning Star...!

All these beautiful attributes are sung between the cantor who chants the verse, while the congregation answers with the refrain; they are presented here in the form of "intercessions..." The Litany concludes with another hymn modeled after *Qoom Faoulos* tune addressed to Christ the "Incarnate God who is born of Mary, the Daughter of David."

This "Litany" is strictly of Maronite composition, modeled after the Syriac methods and reflecting the style of the seventeenth century. In reviewing its content, one finds genuine Maronite expression of Marian theology, imbued with Sacred Scriptures, which our fathers and forefathers have cultivated well. This litany takes us to the heart of the Maronite Marian Tradition, which is far from borrowed and empty hymns that contain neither the spirituality of the Sacred Scriptures nor the deep theological thoughts, let alone their contradiction to the authentic theology of the Church.

The text of the Litany is as follows:

Mary, intercede for your servants   **and have mercy on us**

O Mother of the most merciful One	and the mercy of our Savior
O Pure Virgin	and temple of our Redeemer
O Paradise who received	the life of the departed
O Ship of the weary	and harbor of the troubled
O Temple who was adorned	by the Lord of creations
O Sweet smelling Rose,	through your aroma we are alive
O Lily of the field	and companion to travelers
O Tower of the Son of Jesse	and haven for the refugees
O High Mountain who has surpassed	the height of Mount Sinai
O Precious Jewel	and cherished pearl
O Grapevine whose wine became	the drink of all believers
O Language who contains	the symbols of the Fathers
O Glory of Jerusalem	and victory of the faithful
O Morning Star	through your light we are guided
O Ladder to whom	Jacob has guided us
O Bush of Moses	and hope of the dying
O Paradise who surpassed	any human descriptions
O Rock from whom	we drank the water of life

O Dome whose height has surpassed   that of Mount Sinai
O Promised Garden   and tent of our Shepherd
O Sun from whom shines   the light for travelers
O Ark of the Lord   and dwelling place of our Savior

O Christ, the Incarnate Lord,
when you appeared in due time from
the Virgin Mary, the daughter of David,
all symbols and promises through her were fulfilled

You have chosen her   and dwelt in her womb,
She became ever purer   and attained salvation

protect us under her extended arms
and grant us to enjoy the intended paradise.

C. O Mother of God... *Ya Umm Allah*

This is a simple hymn chanted by a soloist on behalf of the praying faithful. The meanings are quite expressive as we come to the "Mother of God, the treasure of mercy...," asking her to intercede to her Son. This hymn is a cry from the heart and is presently on the lip and tongue of every Maronite to the point where some people have called it the "Maronite National Anthem." It is one of those hymns that unites all Maronites around the world, not only in the churches but also in the homes.

The text of this hymn is as follows:

O Mother of God, O compassionate one,
O treasure of mercy and assistance,
you are our refuge and our hope,
intercede for us and have mercy on our departed.

D. Although Your Body... *Wa Inn Kana Jismookey*

This hymn is translated from Syriac and adapted from the Maronite Liturgical Prayer (the Wednesday hymn of incense of the ninth hour found in the weekly *Sheheemto*). It is characterized by its spiritual depth and genuine belief in the Virgin Mary who was assumed body and soul into Heaven. It consists of the longing of the troubled faithful who trusts that his petition will be answered. It is a perfect sample of Syriac hymns composed of four strophes that are very simple in expression yet very rich in meaning.

The text of this Hymn is as follows:

Although your body is far from us, O our Virgin Mother, your prayers will accompany us, will remain with us and will sustain us.

For the sake of Him Who has honored you above all creation, and who appeared from you in the flesh; beseech Him on behalf of sinners to grant them mercy forever and ever.

You are our Mother and our hope; you are our glory and our refuge; intercede for us to your Son so that through His compassion He may forgive our sins.

O compassionate Mother, filled with every grace, do not abandon us. Rather, save us, your servants, so that we may glorify you forever and ever.

CHAPTER X

Mary in the Maronite
Theological Thought

After having discussed the Liturgical texts in the Prayer of the Hours, in the *Qurbono* and in the paraliturgy of the Procession, and after having addressed the Church Fathers and the Ecumenical Councils, with a long discussion of Saint Ephrem, we can draw a conclusion with some constant ideas about the Virgin Mary and the Maronites. We did not find one particular type of an ancient Maronite Marian theology, nor did we find a thorough study about the Blessed Virgin Mary in the writings of our revered Church Fathers. However, we have barely scratched the surface of the Marian Liturgical texts. From these diverse texts we can conclude the basic thoughts through which our forebears have honored, our Lady, the Blessed Virgin Mary.

These texts may not be exclusively Maronite in nature, but this makes no difference! Why should we make the Maronites "unique species" in the paradise of God? The Maronites are from this scattered Syriac Antiochene East. If the centuries were harsh on them so as to destroy their monasteries along with their cultural and educational centers, then, they have become the remaining minority who sold everything they have in order to purchase the one precious pearl. We find that, what was left from the Maronites themselves, and what they made "Maronite" for their spiritual nourishment, is ample theological material to give us a clear and complete idea about their Marian thoughts and their love for the Virgin Mary that may have grown with them to the point of "worship"!

The Maronites are the fruit of this long journey of ecumenical struggle. From the beginning, they have had the openness of the Antiochene East and, at the same time, they possess a wide range of typical relations in all directions. This is why they could not help but adopt from both, East and West, what corresponded with their basic belief which is stemming from the person of Christ in His two natures, divine and human. They had held on to their belief without arrogance. Therefore, their Marian thoughts were always connected with the basic belief which is based on the one person of Jesus Christ and opened to the entire Universal Church.

We have chosen the Syriac Maronite Liturgical texts preceding the tenth century, which means that they preceded the destruction of the Monastery of Saint Maron. Most of these texts are Syriac in origin, not translated from the Greek Christian tradition. Although these texts were nourished by the Syriac Fathers such as Ephrem, James, Rabbula and others, they are nonetheless, spiritual and intellectual meditations that were not kept in the books of hermits and anchorites. But they were spread to the churches where the faithful have taken them as spiritual nourishment and where they have become a prayer supplication, a litany recited and a sung hymn. Is theology made only for students and researchers? Is it only to be preserved in large encyclopedic volumes preserved in libraries? The best and strongest theology is the one lived by the Christian people. It has been said: "tell me what you pray, I will tell you in what you believe."

It is from these prayers that we have established our belief about the Virgin Mary. From these basic premises we are able to present the Maronite Marian theology that is expressed in the following thoughts:

1. Mary is the "Mother of God"

God, through His infinite wisdom, has drawn the Divine plan for our salvation through the incarnation of the Son and at the same time He willed that Mary be His Mother. The Annunciation and the Incarnation cannot be separated. In the Christian belief, Mary and her Son are not separated. The Church defined this one belief through the Incarnation and the Birth of Jesus who is the only Son of the Most High and the Son of Mary. These thoughts are common and numerous in the Maronite prayers. All of these prayers proclaim that Mary is the Mother of God:

> "Blessed are you, O daughter of David, because you are worthy of being the Mother of God, for you have carried in your womb the Most Powerful One, He who carries heaven and earth."
>
> (adopted from the first hymn of Sunday evening prayer)

> "O Lord Jesus, protect your Church which is adorned in faith. Heresies have attacked her but did not change her faith. Arius, the cursed serpent, attacked her, she crushed his head. After him, the wicked Nestorius, also attacked her, she cursed him along with his teachings. She responded saying: All you who pretend knowledge, your teachings are deceitful; Isaiah is more honest than you, for he wrote about me: Mary is the Mother of God."
>
> (adopted from the first hymn of Sunday evening prayer)

> "Who can possibly simplify the praises of the Blessed Virgin Mary, the Mother of God, who is full of grace...! Blessed are you, because you became the Mother of the Eternal One who is begotten from the Father..., the Mother of the Creator..., the Mother of the Hidden One..."
>
> (adopted from the Sedro of the first watch of Wednesday night prayer)

> "O Jesus Christ, Lord of all, You dwelt in the womb of your Mother Mary who is without blemish, and who truly is the Mother of God and not as the heresy claims... She alone was called 'the Mother of God'..."
>
> (adopted from the *Sedro* of the first watch of Thursday night prayer, and preserved from a seventh or eighth century manuscript)

2. Mary is the Virgin and the Ever-Virgin

In the *Qurbono* there is a perpetual commemoration for Mary as the "Ever-Virgin." In the *Sedro* of the Liturgy of the Word as well as in the first watch of the Sunday evening prayer we read:

> "As we praise and glorify with spiritual hymns, the Ever-Virgin Mary, Mother of God..."

The Virgin Mary is also mentioned in the *Anaphora* of *Sharrar*: "We remember particularly, and by name, the Blessed and Ever-Virgin Mary, Mother of God."

In many such prayers about this topic, Mary has fulfilled the prophecy of Isaiah who says: "The virgin will conceive and bear a son and will name him Emmanuel." It is worth noting what was mentioned earlier that the simple Syriac translation used the term *Olmo* in Isaiah to mean "virgin" in Syriac. That is why the "virginity of Mary" need not be a doubting issue "neither before nor after." Words such as "Virgin," "Ever-Virgin," "Virgin Spouse" and "Virgin Mother" fill the Maronite prayers.

3. Mary has accomplished the Sayings of the Prophets

The view of Syriac Fathers and their teachings was based on the symbols and the sayings of the Prophets. This is viewed in light of the salvific journey from the beginning until Christ. Just as these salvific symbols had been fulfilled in Christ, the second Adam, therefore, many of them had also been fulfilled in Mary, the "second Eve." Mary is the center of these symbols that have occurred in the Old Testament:

> "The bones of all the Prophets stir with joy in their tombs at the memorial of the Blessed Virgin, because the mysteries of their sayings have been fulfilled in Him, who was born from her."
>
> (adopted from the Sunday sundown prayer)

> "All Prophets have envisioned you in their symbols, O Virgin Mary, who became the Mother of God."
>
> (adopted from the *Etro* of the Sunday sundown prayer)

> "Moses has likened you to the Bush; David, your father, to the Jar; Gideon to the Fleece; Solomon to Paradise; Jacob the venerable, to the Ladder; Noah to the Ship of Salvation and Abraham to the glorified dwelling place..."
>
> (adopted from the first hymn of Wednesday night prayer)

"She is the one after whom the symbols of the saintly Prophets have been modeled. All foretold events have been fulfilled and accomplished through you."

(adopted from the *Sedro* of the first watch of Friday night prayer)

"O Blessed Virgin, Mother of the Only Son; the Holy Mountain upon which the divine fire ignited; the bush which was not consumed; the fortified tower in which dwelt the King of glory, the Blessed Vine who carried the precious grape..."

(adopted from the *Sedro* of the first watch of Saturday night prayer)

4. Mary and the Trinity

Throughout the divine salvific journey, the Lord has chosen her from the beginning to have a distinguished role. She has a special place of honor with God. She is connected with the three persons of the Holy Trinity: the "Father has chosen her, the Son dwelt in her, and the Spirit sanctified her." As she is called in the litany entitled "We worship You O Our Savior," Mary is: the "Daughter of the Father, the Mother of the Son and the Spouse of the Holy Spirit."

As we return to the Syriac texts of the *Sheheemto* we find the following:

"Glory to the Father who chose the humble daughter; worship to the Son, who appeared from her in humility and thanksgiving to the Spirit who filled her with richness and great treasures."

(adopted from the *Bo'ooto* of the first watch of Sunday night prayer)

"Glory to the Father, who chose her as a Mother to His only Son; worship to the Son, who took flesh from her in holiness and thanksgiving to the Spirit, who glorified the day of her memory..."

(adopted from the first *Bo'ooto* of the watch of the Wednesday night prayer)

"Glory to the Father, who chose Mary from among all nations; worship to the Son, who dawned from her in holiness and

thanksgiving to the Spirit, who purified her and made her his dwelling place..."
(adopted from the *Bo'ooto* of the first watch of the Saturday night prayer)

5. Mary has the Highest Place in Heaven and on Earth

Mary is the embrace of all nations and all generation. All creation in heaven and on earth calls her blessed, because she became the Mother of the Most High, she became a "second heaven," even higher than the heavens.

"Blessed are you Mary, because you have become the Mother of the Only Light who is one person of the Holy Trinity;

Blessed are you Mary, because you have become the Mother of the true Hope who never deceives through His promises;

Blessed are you Mary, because you have become the Mother of the Mighty One whose glory has filled heaven and earth."
(adopted from the *Sedro* of the first watch of Wednesday night prayer)

"She is the one who was exalted above all creation, because the Word of Life took flesh from her; She is the one who became the Holy of Holies and the dwelling place of her High Priest... Mary, you who are the beatitude of the Prophets, the joy of the Apostles, the crown of the Martyrs, the pride of the heavenly hosts, ..."
(adopted from the *Sedro* of the first watch of Friday night prayer)

"The Virgin Mary appeared on earth like a new Sun, for the Sun of Justice, whose name has existed before the world began, has dawned from her."
(adopted from the hymn of the Sunday morning prayer "He who abides...")

"If I called you a new heaven, then Heaven is lower than you, because He, of whom the heavens are filled, has dawned from you."
(adopted from the hymn of Thursday night prayer)

"Blessed are you, O Mary, and blessed is your humble soul,
because your blessedness is higher than all the blessed..."
(adopted from the *Bo'ooto* of the first watch of Sunday night prayer)

6. Mary intercedes for us with her Son

The following prayers reflect a blend of petitions and supplications to
the one who has earned a "special favor with her Son." Therefore,
words fall short when testimonials are expressed in this regard.
Suffice it here to mention a couple of testimonials which clearly and
truly express this subject.

"...O Blessed Virgin Mary, petition your Son who took flesh
from you and divinized us, Who humbled himself and exalted
us in order to adorn us with virtue... so that we may attain the
heavenly realms."
(adopted from the *Sedro* of the first watch of Saturday night prayer)

"Because she alone has earned your favor and never returned
disappointed since she is the Mother of God. The pure one,
through whom and with whom we offer you our petitions..."
(adopted from the *Sedro* of the first watch of the Monday night prayer)

The Church supplications offered to God, in many of the Syriac
prayers, are addressed to Christ. At the same time, they are petitions
to the Mother of God the Word, to intercede for us with her Son who
has dawned from her, so that we may receive, through her, what we
ask of Him.

7. Mary was assumed into Heaven in Body and Soul

If one were to search the old texts of the *Sheheemto*, one would find
the memorial of the Virgin Mary's Assumption, body and soul, just as
the popular hymn describes it "although your body is far from us"
(the *Etro* of the first watch of the Wednesday prayer). Furthermore,
one would find numerous prayers about Mary's Assumption in the
Proper of the Virgin Mary and in the Proper of the Feast of the
Assumption. The *Sedro* of the feast day of the Assumption has been
discussed in the chapter of the Maronite Liturgical Prayer. Belief in

the Assumption did not wait until 1950 to be officially proclaimed as dogma in the Maronite Church, but has entered it prior to the tenth century because of the prominent influence that has been spread since the fifth century.

8. Mary is the "Immaculate Conception"

Proclaimed by Pope Pius IX on 1854, this dogma means that the Virgin Mary is free from the Original Sin with which were labeled our first parents and the entire human race. In a special favor, God preserved Mary from this common curse. Indeed, we could find neither the concept of the Original Sin the way it is understood today, nor the perception of being preserved from it. However, Saint Ephrem, and later all the Syriac liturgical texts, clarified how Mary became the "dwelling place of the Holy Spirit," the "undefiled Mother" and the purest of all creation. In conclusion about the "Pure and Undefiled" we could not find more expressive terms than the following bouquet of prayers:

> "Hail Mary, you are the fortified city who was never defiled by sin!
> Hail Mary, you are the bride of the King of Kings!"
> (adopted from the *Sedro* of the first watch of Tuesday night prayer)

> "O Lord, You humbled yourself to become one of us. You dwelt in the womb of the Virgin, which was sanctified by the Holy Spirit, the womb of Your Mother, the Blessed Virgin Mary who is without blemish, and who surpasses heaven in glory and height."
> (adopted from the *Sedro* of the first watch of Thursday night prayer)

> "Come forth all of you, peoples and nations of the earth. Let us sing glory to the Father who sent His Son to Mary; let us give thanks to the Son who was born from her in purity; and let us worship the Spirit who preserved her from harm. Therefore, her memory is honored in the depths and in the heights, may her prayer sustain us."
> (adopted from the *Etro* of the first watch of Friday night prayer)

CHAPTER XI

Mary in the Maronite Icon

The "icon" or the "picture" as called today is at the heart of the devotion, both the liturgy and the life of the people. We prefer the term "icon" over "picture" because it is the authentic expression of this reality. Being translated from the Greek term "ikun," its pronunciation remains in our common language as "icon." Some of the Maronite liturgical books still use the term "Icon:" For example in the 1909 Edition of the *Book of Rituals*, we find the "Benediction with the icon of the Holy Rosary" on page 243, the "Benediction with the icon of Saint Maron..." on page 460 and the "Benediction with the icon of the Scapular of Our Lady" on page 267. However, the commonly used term at the present time is "picture," thus the "picture of Our Lady" or the "Benediction with the picture..." If we were to search old Maronite resources, both manuscripts and print, we would always find the term "icon" just as it is printed in the introduction of the 1624 Maronite *Sheheemto*.

What is important here is that Our Lady must be venerated through her picture or icon in a widespread, well-known and popular devotion: the picture is venerated from far or near, in front of it there are lighted candles, burnt incense, a blessing is received from its "oil lamp" et cetera...!

In the Maronite Church, there is a designated place for the icon of the Virgin Mary. It has a special veneration throughout the rituals. It is located on the left side of the altar, whereas the Book of the Gospel is on the right. It is usually placed in front of the railing that separates the holy of holies from the rest of the church, so that people can have easy access for veneration since they are not permitted to enter the sanctuary. In the introduction of the 1624 *Sheheemto* we read the following:

> "In the beginning of the prayer (morning and evening...) the priest stands at the entrance of the sanctuary, makes the sign of the cross, the faithful do likewise, he does the Metanies... and the Trisagion (thrice holy God)..., he uncovers his head, venerates the icon of (Our Lady), the Gospel Book and then proceeds to the lectern..."

These rubrics talk about the incensing of the Book of the Gospel, and the "incensing of the icon." This tradition is still practiced today whereby, the Gospel Book is placed on the right lectern while the "icon of Our Lady" on the left, but in front of the railing. In the small churches, the icon was moved inside the sanctuary, then it was hung on the wall to the left of the altar, just as it is in most of the churches. Today's practice in bringing out the "picture of Our Lady" from the sacristy to the altar for veneration is non-traditional and non-liturgical. Only the picture, which is exposed in the church, is the one that must be honored and venerated by the faithful, and not the one that is preserved in the "storage room."

In addition to the "icon of Our Lady" that is found in all the Maronite Churches, there are special churches consecrated to "Our Lady" under various names. There is a large number of Maronite churches named after Our Lady. We conclude from a short survey conducted in the Lebanese eparchies that at least "one fourth" of the churches are named after "Our Lady;"[21] the same statistics are reflected in the Maronite Eparchy of Cyprus, which is presently called the Eparchy of Antelias.[22]

Each of these Marian Churches has "icons" and there is a special veneration to this or that miraculous "picture." Reviewing the history of these Marian churches in Lebanon, we find a special history to each church and to each icon along with popular stories which entered the history and the life of the Lebanese society from

---

[21] Father Boutros Daou, *The Maronite Churches of the Virgin Mary in Lebanon and in the World*, 1988.

[22] *Guide to the Maronite Eparchy of Cyprus*, 1980. (23 out of 85 churches are named after Our Lady).

ancient time.[23] We shall later present a study about the most famous Maronite churches that are named after "Our Lady," but first we must address two important issues:

- Do the Maronites have a special type of Marian pictures or icons?

- Is this type still preserved or has it been obliterated?

In order to address these two topics, one must refer to the ancient Maronite history, consult the archives of the present icons and check the history of the religious iconographic art, which may take us directly to the origins of our Maronite art.

We are not going to engage in a serious and thorough study about a Maronite iconographic art. However, looking at some revealing resources, we shall present the issue and open the door for research ascertaining that we have a special inherited art deeply rooted in our Syriac Maronite Tradition, which is necessary to revisit and discover.

We shall first present what we have at hand then later refer to the ancient history:

1. The Present Maronite icons in the Churches.
2. The History of the icons.

1. The Present Maronite Icons in the Churches

In each Maronite church named after Our Lady in Lebanon we find one or several icons for her. Their number exceeds six hundred in Lebanon alone.[24] The majority is preserved from the eighteenth, the nineteenth and the twentieth centuries.

To the expert, it appears that these icons are of West-European inspiration that were brought into Lebanon by missionaries since the seventeenth century. The Maronites themselves may have imported them either from Rome and France or they may have imitated them.

---

[23] H. Jalabert, *The Holy Virgin in Lebanon.* Beirut, 1955.
[24] Father Boutros Daou, *The Maronite Churches of the Virgin Mary in Lebanon and in the World,* 1988. Preliminary survey, (pp. 11-14).

Recently, however, "statues" of the Virgin Mary have become quite popular, making them the most recent import from Europe.

Two Roman pictures have influenced this Maronite collection the most: (a) the picture of Our Lady which is preserved in the Cathedral of Santa Maria Maggiore in Rome, known as the picture of the "Salvation of the Roman people;" and (b) the picture of "Our Lady of the Road." In the eighteenth century, Italian as well as French pictures were added to this collection, while several pictures of the "Immaculate Conception" surfaced around the nineteenth century. However, "Maronite" artists in Lebanon were scarce during that particular period, and if there were any, they may have copied or imitated them.

Today, the Maronites do not possess one particular type of icon, Marian or other. But our churches and homes are filled with pictures from different sources and countries and from all kinds of Western schools of iconography, to the point where the type of the true religious "icon" is lost. Instead, they have simply adopted artistic "pictures" replicating the prototype of Italian and French schools of iconography.

2. The History of the Icons

There are numerous junctures in the history of Maronite icons just as there are for the Maronite people themselves, along with their cultural facets, be they religious, educational or social. The identified junctures for the iconographic art that we have today are as follows:

- **First:**   The Gospel of Rabbula, 586 A.D.;
- **Second:** The Icon of *Ileej* from the tenth century;
- **Third:**   The Mural Paintings of the Maronite churches under the influence of the Crusades, from the twelfth to the thirteenth century;
- **Fourth:** The Old Preserved Maronite Icons from the seventeenth and the eighteenth centuries.

We shall first present these "junctures" of iconographic art that are in our possession in order to infer a possible conclusion.

First: The Gospel of Rabbula,[25] 586 A.D.

We shall not even try to argue whether this manuscript is Syriac or Maronite, it is actually Syro-Maronite. When the paintings and writing of the manuscript were completed in 586 A.D., the Western Syriac and the Maronite Syriac art were synonymous. From the eleventh century on, this manuscript became the property of the Maronite Patriarchate and its exclusive use for over five hundred years. It was, without a doubt, the source of meditation and artistic inspiration.

In this illustrated Gospel there are numerous pictures dedicated to the Virgin Mary: in some essential pictures she is standing by herself, in some others she appears with other people. They are as follows:

> **"The Virgin Mary, Mother of God":** Mary is standing, carrying Jesus on her left arm as He carries the Book of the Gospel over his right hand. Her face has an oval shape and there is large halo over her head. She is dressed in a long golden robe and stands on an ornamented platform decorated with precious stones. The "Virgin Mary" of Rabbula is the "Mother of God" who deserves to be venerated by the faithful. There are numerous and lengthy studies about this icon situating it in the traditional Syriac surrounding as depicted in Saint Luke. According to researchers, she is of the Syriac origin of Edessa, which later spread to Eastern and Western Churches. It could be an enlightening experience, for some researchers, if they delve a little more deeply in this subject[26].

> **The Annunciation:** The Virgin Mary stands as the "Mother of God" who is "full of grace" as she converses with the Angel.

> **The Nativity of Jesus:** Mary in the forefront pointing out to the Child.

---

[25] -- This Manuscript is preserved in the Library of Florence. Plut. I. 56 Cecchelli (C.), Furlani (J.) Salmi, *The Rabbula Gospels.* Facsimile Edition, Olten-Urs-Graf, 1959.
 -- Father Boutros Daou, Maronite Ecclesial Painting, The Gospel of Rabbula and Its Icons, *The History of the Maronites,* Volume VII, 1987.
[26] -- Jules Le Roy, *The Painted Syriac Manuscripts,* Paris, Genther, 1964.
 -- Antoine Lammens, *The Syriac Miniatures of the Rabbula Codex,* (a non-published paper) The Holy Spirit University, Kaslik, Lebanon, 1975.

Cana of Galilee: Jesus and His Mother are in the Center.

The Crucifixion and the Resurrection: To the right of the Crucified Jesus stands "His Mother" dressed in a dark garment with a "halo" over her head. Mary also appears in the scene of the "Resurrection of Jesus" and that is quite clear.

The Ascension: The Virgin Mary stands in the middle surrounded by two angels and the Apostles.

Pentecost: The Virgin Mary is standing and surrounded by the twelve Apostles while the Holy Spirit descends on her and on all of them.

These Marian faces in Rabbula could use some very serious study because they are the most ancient icons known about Mary, not only in the Syriac but in the entire Eastern Tradition.

Second: The Icon of *Ileej*

It was through an absolute Marian miracle that a Maronite icon of Our Lady was discovered. This icon dates back to the tenth century and was preserved in the church of *Ileej*.

Ileej is located in the valley of Mayfouq, which, back then, was considered in the district of Batroun, but at the present time, it is in the district of Jbeil. It served as the location of the Maronite Patriarchal See from the beginning of the twelfth until the middle of the fifteenth century. It is one of the oldest locations for the Maronite Patriarchs. After the Patriarchal See was moved from the Monastery of Saint Maron, on the Orontes River, it settled in Kfarhay, a town in the Batroun region, then in Yanouh, near Akoura and later in *Ileej*.

The Meaning of the Icon

She is the Virgin Mary, the "Mother of God" who carries the Child Jesus on her left arm. She is standing straight and holding Jesus. It is the "Icon of the Mother of God" from whom the Word took flesh. She is standing while her hand is extended in a blessing-like movement. Edessa may very well be the source of these Marian icons known as the "guide on the road." This type of art was never under the influence of Byzantine art, but the Babylonian art is more predominant in the hand of the Virgin Mary. The main reason is that the size of the hand is much larger than it should be; this is typical in Babylonian art because of the importance of the hand that gives the blessing. In the Babylonian mythology there is a picture for the mother goddess which is mother-earth from whom man was born! The hand of goddess mother-earth plays a great role in the "Creation of Man."

The last indication that it belongs to Syro-Aramaic tradition is the appearance of the sun and the moon in the upper part of the icon. Sun and moon are two symbols, from the Aramaic art, associated with the goddess of fertility.

What is quite characteristic about the icon of the "The Mother of Good Counsel" in the Syriac art is the fact that the left hand of the Virgin Mary does not show. It is hidden under the veil with which she wraps the Child, while his face appears to be facing the onlooker.

The History of the Icon

There is a "miraculous" story about the Icon of Our Lady of *Ileej* that must be told[27] and it goes as follows:

In 1980 the Icon of Our Lady, which was housed in *Ileej*, was brought to the art workshop of the Carmelite convent in Harissa for repair. It was preserved in a glass box. The dimensions of the icon are 149 x 112 centimeters. It was painted on a rectangular canvas consisting of three pieces, measuring 42 + 42 + 42 centimeters. One part of the third piece, which was originally 42 centimeters, was cut off. The Icon had sustained some burns and humidity damages. The artistic lines of the Icon of Our Lady indicate that it is in fact

[27] Information taken from a research study preserved in the convent of the Carmelite Nuns in Harissa, Kessrouwan, Lebanon.

Maronite with Italian influence from the end of the eighteenth century. The Virgin Mary carries Jesus on her left arm while her right reaches over her left and over the knee of the Child.

After the nuns have begun restoring this badly damaged icon, there appeared to be many colored layers under the main surface. Stages of scientific research about this icon started, they are as follows:

- The X-rays photography began in June of 1984. Old stratified layers appeared under the actual surface.

- The supervision of X-rays and infrared radiations.

- Chemical solutions, in Lebanon and abroad, were applied on some specimen taken from the icon between 1983 and 1986

- Numerous researches in advanced scientific laboratories were done in France.

When these various layers of the icon were closely examined, a very old layer was found containing painting materials initially used not on a canvas but on a mural. When this extensive research was completed on June 1986, it revealed clearly the following findings:

This modern icon of Our Lady hides underneath its initial surface, nine different layers before it reveals the icon of the Virgin Mary. This is a very old mural type of iconography belonging to the Maronite Syriac art and dating back to the tenth century. Three crucial signs prove these artistic findings:

A. The Shape of the Icon
B. The Material used for painting
C. The Method of painting

A. The Shape of the Icon

Returning to the Syriac iconographic art, and to everything that researchers may possess, we find plenty of this "Syriac" type of icons which is still preserved in Rome itself since it was under the influence of Syriac art, between the sixth and the seventh centuries[28]. Among the remaining iconographic art from the churches of Syria II, there is a seventh century icon of the Virgin Mary, in the same shape, and is still preserved in Calabrea, southern Italy. During this period the Maronites sculpted the Virgin Mary with the Child Jesus, on stones above their church doors, in the same shape that appears in the Icon of *Ileej*.[29]

This type of icon is strong and famous in the East; it was attributed to Saint Luke and originated in Edessa. From there, it branched out to Byzantium, Armenia, Russia and even Rome, then later Egypt and Ethiopia. As for its return from Rome to the Maronites, it was by way of a very old picture that is preserved in the Cathedral of Santa Maria Maggiore, which is entitled "Salvation of the Roman People" and may date back to the ninth century. The Jesuits brought it to the Maronites throughout their missions since the end of the sixteenth century. This icon has spread among the famous Maronite churches that were named after Our Lady such as: Our Lady of the Hill in Deir El-Qamar, Our Lady of the Gate in Jbeil, Our Lady of the Towers in Ghazir and so many others. We find this picture in the churches of Our Lady in villages such as the church of Tameesh, the church of Our Lady in Ein El-Kharroubeh, Our Lady in Baskinta, Our Lady of Howqa, Our Lady of Beqaa Kafra and the old church of Our Lady in Tannoureen.

B. The material used for painting

After studying the employed materials it is evident that the icon of *Ileej* dates back to the tenth century, which was

[28]   Andre Grabar, *The First Christian Art*. Paris, 1966.
[29] -- J. Lassus, *Christian Sanctuaries of Syria*. Paris, 1944.
   -- H. Butler, *Early Churches in Syria*. Princeton University, 1929.

actually a "fresco." This means that it was originally painted on a wall and then later, through special methods familiar to that particular era, it was copied onto canvas, which made it much easier to move from place to place. This type of copying procedures may have been common during the tenth century. It is a known fact that the final destruction of the Monastery of Saint Maron, the Patriarchal See, was around the middle of the tenth century! Could the Maronites have brought with them the icon of the Virgin Mary to the new Patriarchal location in Mount Lebanon?

C. The method of painting

This type of iconography is based on measurements used by architectural methods inspired from Christ's initial letters in Greek such as IX. The scope herein does not allow for details, however, through the invention of such type of iconography, the artist is able to restore parts of any particular icon that may have been erased with time. In fact, this is what helped the Carmelite nuns restore the icon of *Ileej* starting from the premise of this basic method.

Summary:

The icon of *Ileej* carries, within its multifaceted layers, the Maronite Syriac history that evolved along with historical and geographic periods which the people have actually lived. In this *Ileej* icon and its various derivatives, we find the original "Maronite icon" which we can still sense through the type of art and icons that have remained with us. Future research studying old icons such as that of Howqa, Qannoubeen, Cyprus and many others, may help us discover, under their modern surfaces, aged icons going back to the Middles Ages and even before.

Third: The Mural Paintings under the influence of the Crusades

Father Youhanna Sader, a monk of the Antonine Order, conducted a recent research about these Maronite churches, in which he discussed frescos in three churches located in the regions of Jbeil and Batroun: (a) the church of Bihdaydat, (b) the church of Mea'ad and (c) the church of Iddeh-Batroun.[30] The research consists of studying these Maronite murals which were under the influence of the iconographic art that was prominent during the period of the Crusades—but inspired from Eastern art and Syriac inscriptions. It is worth noting these striking frescos of the Blessed Virgin Mary. The icon of Our Lady of "Supplication" and that of Our Lady of the "Annunciation" in Bihdaydat both go back to the end of the twelfth century. The icon of the "Burial of the Virgin Mary" in the church of Iddeh-Batroun dates back to the thirteenth century. This study did not include many famous murals in other churches, in the grottos of Qadisha and in numerous other locales that are waiting yet to be discovered.

In addition to these Marian mural paintings, one was discovered in 1941 on the wall of a church in the old street market of Beirut, dating back to the period of the crusades, and is described as follows:

> "A Virgin is standing wearing a green garment, carrying on her left arm the Child Jesus. Her right arm is raised toward the right hand of the Child who is giving a blessing."[31]

This type resembles the traditional shape mentioned in the method of both Rabbula and Ileej, following the same iconographic art found in the icon of the "Mother of Good Counsel."

Fourth: The Old Preserved Maronite Icons

It is necessary to familiarize ourselves with the icons that are in our churches today, especially those that are close to the traditional Maronite type. In these old icons that are preserved until today in

---

[30] Youhanna Sader, *Mural Paintings in the Medieval Maronite Churches.* Beirut, 1987.
[31] Jean Lauffray, *Forms and Monuments of Beirut, Bulletin of the Beirut Museum.*
    Vol. VIII, 1946-48, (p. 9).

Maronite churches, in Lebanon and in Cyprus, we find imitation of the *Ileej* type but following the Roman art methodology. However, this has created an undesirable mixture that requires us to go back to the origins, in order to rid our art from all kinds of foreign influence so that we may have today the authentic "Maronite icon," which is inspired from our own tradition and from our own history. Further, it is necessary to study the old preserved icons that we possess today, those that are known, and those that are yet to be discovered.

Conclusion

Do the Maronites have a special iconographic art?

The answer is yes. However, we must discover it and define its parameters. We have found the Maronite path: It is Rabbula from 586; it is *Ileej* from the tenth century; it is the mural paintings of those Maronite churches; it is the old preserved Maronite icons that are inspired from the above mentioned Eastern art.

This path, rather these paths, of Maronite art, along with many that might yet be discovered, will certainly enrich our churches and provide artists and knowledgeable people with an abundance of wealth to help them create an authentic Maronite "icon" to Our Lady, the most honorable Virgin Mary, Mother of God.

Studio of Maronite Iconography in Cyprus

We have established, in Nicosia, an icon painting studio for the Maronite Eparchy of Cyprus modeled after the iconographic art of the Syriac Maronite tradition which is preserved in ancient Syriac miniatures of the Rabbula Codex.

We have already published two books about these icons a substantial number of which is dedicated to the Virgin Mary.[32]

---

[32] -- The Maronite Icons – *Modern Sacred Art*. Sader Publishers, Beirut, 1999
  -- The Marontie Icons – *Saints of the Maronite Church*. Sader Publishers, Beirut, 2003

CHAPTER XII

Mary in Some Maronite Shrines

As we continue our presentation of the Virgin Mary in the Maronite Church, we shall extend our study to a very important topic that shakes the heart of the devout Maronite people. This topic covers churches, shrines and places of worship consecrated to God that are named after Our Lady, the Virgin Mary. These holy places resemble the old temples in which dwells the divine power: The church of Our Lady is a sacred temple to which pilgrims come offering their prayers and supplications and asking for miracles!

As far as people are concerned, the holy locales named after Our Lady and the saints are consecrated to God who dwells in them with His saints, as if they are a second heaven about which countless stories and legends are told.

Holy sites of pilgrimages in the East were, and still are, places upon which the Spirit descends, in which souls are sanctified and people are healed from sickness of body and soul. Just as the hermitage of Saint Maron was a popular site of pilgrimage for throngs of peoples back then, so have the famous Marian churches and shrines become for our times.

The renowned historian, Theodoret of Cyrrhus, gave one of the most beautiful descriptions about the shrines of the fifth century when he wrote:

> "There, in those shrines..., people who have good health pray to keep it, the sick pray to be healed of their afflictions, those who do not have children pray to have them, barren women

pray to become mothers...! Whether or not these prayers have been answered, this is revealed through the offerings left there: some leave the picture of an eye, others offer a picture of a hand in silver or in gold, and God, in his mercy, accepts our humble offerings because He looks, not at the value of the gift, but toward the person who offers the gift..."[33]

The shrine has its own special character, the church of Our Lady has a special place of honor in the soul of the Maronite person, but the sacredness of the "Shrine" has its own gleaming radiance far beyond a mere passing visit. These pilgrim churches served as a tremendous guide and source of sustenance during tragedies, displacements, migrations, sicknesses and wars, and marked the people with an indelible spiritual seal to maintain the faith.

The shrine Our Lady of Lebanon in Harissa plays a very important role in all aspects of peoples' lives. In their view, she will "protect Lebanon" in the future just as she has protected it until today. When we see tens of thousands of visitors go to Harissa, especially during feasts and memorials of the Virgin Mary, we understand that there is a special place for the church of the Virgin Mary in the heart of every Maronite. In fact, what draws a faithful person to her shrine is the Lady who is present in his heart, the Lady who is in the church of his village or home, which he brings with him to Harissa.

Lebanon has an abundance of churches named after the Virgin Mary, not only among the Maronites, but among all Christians where the number exceeds thirteen hundred churches and three thousand altars. The Maronite Marian churches alone surpass six hundred.[34] In our short presentation of these Marian churches and shrines, we shall mention some of them that are spread all around Lebanon and cover the historical periods from the early Christian centuries until today. We shall briefly mention them only because they provide us, historically and geographically, with a general idea about honoring the Virgin Mary. Therefore, churches were chosen from the south to the north of Lebanon, beginning with the oldest and ending with the newest—six churches modeled after six different examples.

---

[33] Theodoret of Cyrrhus, *Sermon 8, the Martyrs*, (P.G. tt. 83, Col. 1032).
[34] Cf. The Statistics of the Marian exhibits in Beit-Meri that are mentioned in the book of Father Gilbert, *The Virgin Mary in Lebanon*. (p. 270).

1. The Church of Our Lady in Tyre

The city of Tyre, in South Lebanon today, is not far from Nazareth, nor is it far from Jesus and His Mother. The Lord visited the land of Tyre and Sidon and cured the daughter of the Canaanite woman. Stories recounted by Saint Epiphanius of Salamis, a fourth century bishop, mention that the Mother of Jesus accompanied him on this particular trip. There are countless stories about numerous locations that the Virgin Mary has visited between Tyre and Sidon.

It is a well known fact that Tyre is a land consecrated by Christ himself, where the Apostles spread the faith and where a Christian community was established since the days of Saint Paul, as the Act of the Apostles tell us (Acts 21: 4-6). In Tyre, the first Christians were persecuted. In Tyre, Origen, the great theologian, was buried in the year 252, where his tomb became a pilgrimage for centuries.

Tyre became the capitol of Christian Phoenicia. The Archbishop of this historic city presided over thirteen eparchies encompassing all of Phoenicia, starting with Arka in the north and reaching Tyre, in the south, with the exception of Beirut (see the Synod of Mount Lebanon, Part 3, Section 4). One of the oldest Christian churches, with the architectural style of a Basilica, was built and consecrated in Tyre by its Archbishop Paulinos, in 314 A.D., long before the churches of Jerusalem, Rome and others came to be. This church, for that particular time in history, was one of the largest and most beautiful in the world, measuring about 280 feet long by 175 feet wide.

It was this church whose name was changed to bear the name of the Virgin Mary after the Council of Ephesus in 431. In this very church many councils were convoked, the most important of which is the Council of Tyre in 518, when the bishops of the region announced their adherence to the Council of Chalcedon and their opposition to the teaching of Severus of Antioch. The chronicles of the fifth ecumenical council, which was convoked in 553, describes the results of the Council of Tyre saying: "The people were gathered outside the church waiting for the bishop to read the decision about accepting the Council of Chalcedon. They took to the streets in demonstration shouting enthusiastically: 'It is the Mother of God who exiled

Severus, who caused trouble for the churches.' "[35] Gradually, through the passing of centuries, Tyre lost its glory... During the period of the Crusades, Tyre gained back its prominence when it became the coronation center of the Crusade Kings, which took place in its famous Cathedral. Then, once again, Tyre lost its notoriety.

In Tyre today there is a church named after Our Lady of Perpetual Help, known as "Our Lady of the Seas" and is built upon an ancient historic site. It is the Cathedral of the Maronite Archbishop of Tyre. The Maronites who were displaced in the fifteenth century from the region of Qannoubeen, and who moved to the region of Bisharry, were displaced again. This time, they migrated to Tyre around the beginning of the nineteenth century where they built this beautiful church. Ancient in tradition yet quite modern, this church of Our Lady is still, to this day, a shrine of pilgrimage to the entire region.

2. The Church of Our Lady in Beirut

Beirut also had experienced the Apostolic preaching through Saint Jude. Mary has been honored in it since the early Christian era and this is, without a doubt, due to the shining period of the Council of Ephesus. A Christian student, who lived in Beirut with Severus of Antioch when they were students at the famous School of Law, in 487, recorded in his diary the following:[36]

> In the evening, after classes, "I would rush to the Church of the Resurrection to pray, from there, I would go to the Church of the Mother of God, which was located inside the city, near the Sea Port. After my prayers, I would take a walk in front of this Church."

This student frequented the church with his classmates to pray and to study the Sacred Scriptures. He tells a story that had actually happened in those days about a group of students who conned people with cheating and sorcery; one day the police arrested them and burnt their books. This incident took place "in front of the Church of the Blessed Virgin Mary, the Mother of God."

---

35 Mansi, *Amplissima Collectio Conciliorum.* t. 8, Col. 1084.
36 The Life of Severus. By Zachariah the Scholastic, *Oriental Patrology.* t. 2, (p. 48).

After the infamous earthquake that destroyed Beirut in 551, the people abandoned the city. However, this ruined church remained a hidden, yet a popular, shrine for a long period of time. People in the inner city were still honoring the Virgin Mary in a special shrine located inside Beirut old street market, called "al-nouriyet" or "saydet al-nouriyet" which translates into "Our Lady of the Light" up until the outbreak of the civil war in 1975. The Crusaders had built a shrine for the Virgin Mary in the same vicinity. The excavations of 1941 revealed a picture of the Virgin Mary on one of the walls.[37] The metropolitan Beirut of today is different from the old Beirut, but the church of "Our Lady of the Gifts," even though fairly modern, still is the church of one of the larger Maronite parishes in the city. It is noteworthy to mention that Beirut is filled with churches named after the Virgin Mary, that belong to other Christian denominations.

3. The Church of Our Lady in Jbeil

In the city of (Byblos), Jbeil today, the church is called "Our Lady of the Gate." The name refers to the Lady, patroness of the city, who stands at the gate to protect it from harm. By Jbeil here, we do not only mean to speak of the city itself but also of the region. Jbeil was the holy city for the Phoenicians, its Lord was Baal and his "Lady" Astarte. A wedding feast was celebrated annually in honor of the Baal and his bride, Adonis and Astarte, processing along the river which originates in "Afqa." Starting in the city and proceeding to the delta of the river, the celebration followed upward to its source in the mountain. After the spread of Christianity in Mount Lebanon and the establishment of the Christian State, the churches of the Virgin Mary, Mother of God, began to replace the temples that were once consecrated to Lady Astarte. From these Phoenician pagan shrines sprung these numerous churches in and around the city of Jbeil and extended from the coastal plains all the way up to Afqa. In the year 399, the Emperor issued a decree ordering the destruction of all pagan temples while John Chrysostom sent missionaries to the Mountains of Phoenicia. This phenomenon was nicely described by Saint Augustine: "People were converting just as fast as the temples." Afqa, the defiled place of Astarte, was destroyed and replaced by a

---

[37] See previous Chapter on the "icon" during the Crusade Period.

church in which the commemoration of the Virgin Mary remains until today.

The churches named after "Our Lady" with the closest location to Afqa were, at one time, the residence of the Maronite Patriarchate. During the tenth century it was "Our Lady of Yanouh." During the eleventh century it was "Our Lady of Abel." Then, it was "Our Lady of Ileej," where the Patriarchs lived under her protection, from 1121 until 1439—a period that lasted over three centuries. Her famous icon, which dates back to the tenth century, has already been discussed in the previous chapter.

In summary, Jbeil, the center of Adonis and Astarte the ancient Baal, has also become a city, a region and a center for the churches of the Virgin Mary, and a long time residence for the Maronite Patriarchate.

4. The Church of Our Lady in Qannoubeen

After the monastic reform that took place in the fourth century, the monks requested to establish a monastery that would serve as headquarter for the hermitages that are spread around the area; the "Monastery" was built and thus, its name in Greek is "Qannoubeen." Based on several sources, Al-Douwaihy claims that hermits, numbered in hundreds, are filling caves and grottos in the Qadeesha Valley. Each hermit lived his own personal way of spirituality and meditation whereas the "Monastery" served as a refuge and a center of the Eucharist for them all. Our Lady has been the "Patroness" of the monastery since its inception in the fifth century. From this monastery young monks started their spiritual life, establishing hermitages in caves and "crevices of the earth," under the protection of the Lady, the neighbor of the Cedars of Lebanon, to which she was likened: "She was exalted like the Cedars in Lebanon."

"Our Lady of Qannoubeen" was a refuge to those monks who fled from the world. In the fifteenth century, it also became a refuge to the Maronite Patriarch who fled from the ruthless and oppressive rulers of the time. He lived with his bishops in this monastery from 1440 until 1830, close to four hundred years.

The largest feast in the Qadeesha Valley was the "Feast of Our Lady" which falls on August 15. Visitors described this feast as the "National Day" when dignitaries, Ambassadors and Consuls General along with the clergy and the people, gathered around the Patriarch for the celebration. In this monastery of Our Lady of Qannoubeen, the first Lebanese Synod was convoked in 1596, in the presence of a papal delegate.

"Qannoubeen" is the symbol and the pilgrimage of Maronite spirituality. To this day, Our Lady of Qannoubeen along with Our Lady of Howqa, in the Qadeesha, witness to the attachment of the Maronites to "Our Lady." These also mark the fact that the majority of the Patriarchal residences were kept under the protection of the "Mother of God." From Qannoubeen, the Patriarch moved to "Our Lady of Bkerke," near Harissa, making it the winter residence while "Our Lady of Deman," near Bisharry, was the summer residence.

5. Our Lady of Bkerke-Harissa

When the Maronite Patriarchs moved to the vicinity of Jounieh toward the end of the eighteenth century, also "Our Lady of Bkerke" was their Patroness. When Patriarch Elias El-Houwayek honored the memorial of the Virgin Mary by celebrating the Golden Jubilee of the proclamation of the Immaculate Conception, Harissa, located close to the residence of the Maronite Patriarchate, was chosen to be the site of this commemoration under the name of "Our Lady of Lebanon." Patriarch El-Houwayek, the forger of modern Lebanon, inaugurated this shrine in 1908.

Today, the shrine of "Our Lady of Lebanon" in Harissa has become the symbol and the pilgrimage site to every one who loves Our Lady. A Basilica, bearing the name of the Virgin Mary, has been built on the site. It is one of the largest churches in Lebanon with a capacity exceeding two thousand seats.

All the churches that are named after the Virgin Mary, be they in Harissa-Bkerke, in Qannoubeen, in Ileej, in Yanouh..., they have preserved and will continue to preserve the love of the Maronites for the Mother of God who, in turn, intercedes to her Son through the influence she has with Him.

6. Our Lady of Perpetual Help in Ain El-Kharroubeh

Our Lady of Perpetual Help is my parish church. In it I was baptized, in it I celebrated my first *Qurbono* and in it I have lived my religious and liturgical life. To her I owe a deep sense of gratitude.

The oldest church is no longer there. However, the icon of the Virgin Mary "Mother of the Light," the artwork of a "Maronite monk from 1763," is the only remaining relic. The fairly recent church that was dedicated in 1882 houses a large picture, dating back to the late nineteenth century, painted by the famous artist Dawood Al-Qurum. The newest church was consecrated on June 13, 2005 and consists of the following complex:

a. A cemetery;

b. A large parish hall measuring 5400 square feet along with meeting rooms around it;

c. The capacity of this new church exceeds six hundred seats. It houses a large painting of Our Lady, replicated by Anthony Ghanim from the previous work of Dawood Al-Qurum, but in a special artistic form. The painting covers the entire apse and the wall behind the altar. It is considered the largest painting of the Virgin Mary on canvas in Lebanon, measuring 315 square feet.

d. A shrine housing a very large statue for the Virgin Mary is mounted on the church roof.

CHAPTER XIII

Mary in the Maronite Family

The family in society is like the cell in the body. If the family is safe, the society is sound. If a disease gets a grip on it, then it is doomed forever.

The family is the life and the nucleus of the Church; it is the small church in the large church. It is the "dwelling place of the living God." It is the temple which is consecrated to the Lord in the image of the soul that is baptized with water and anointed with Chrism.

The Maronite family was likened to the oil jar of Elijah, blessed by God no matter how harsh the times and how painful the centuries have been to her! It is known by the multiplicity of her children and famous for its devotion and trust in God, "under the watchful eye of the Virgin Mary."

The Maronite home was an image of a church, nestled in a mountain, consecrated to God, bearing the name of the Virgin Mary. It always prided itself with an "altar" or an icon for the Virgin Mary, before which one finds candles, incense, oil and flowers! In the evening, a gorgeous voice along with a beautiful melody sings the hymn of *Ya Umm Allah...*, which means "O Mother of God...," while the choir, old and young, answers in bursting joy and pride the hymn of *wa inn kana jismookey ba'idan minna...; utlubey min wahidik lee ajlina...* which means "Although your body is far from us...; Petition your only Son for us..."

The Virgin Mary is present in our home at every hour and moment and with every one, young or old, as if she is in Cana of Galilee sharing our joys and sorrows. At night, the mother whispers to her the family concerns and every morning, the father looks toward her with trust and faith. To her, the youths raise their eyes with love and hope, while the little children kneel at her feet with innocence and confidence.

It is no wonder why the icon of the Virgin Mary has been our refuge and our hope in every period on the journey of life: when expecting a child, through the safe delivery of a worried mother, in sickness, in despair, in traveling and before departure...! Be it traveling in this life or before departure to everlasting life, the icon of the Virgin Mary is the companion on the road of life.

There is a lofty place for the Virgin Mary in the Liturgy of the family in which one finds a Marian procession:

- In the ceremony of Betrothal of a couple, the blessing of the priest is there: "Through the prayers of the Blessed Virgin Mary, Mother of God."

- In the ceremony of Crowning, along with the flowers on the heads of the bride and groom and their witnesses, the icon of the Virgin Mary is processed around the church.

- In the ceremony of Baptism! In spite of the official text which is dedicated to the hymn of the procession, the Maronites refused but to process with the icon of the Virgin Mary and to chant her hymns.

- Even in the Funeral Services as well as in the Service of Incense, the Virgin Mary is depicted as the "ship of the new covenant, she passed on earth and granted life to the dead."

Mary is a friend to every member of the family to the point where the common saying applies—they are all "Marians." Thus, the mother is a member of the local "Marian Sorority" which is a part of a larger consortium of sororities of the Virgin Mary that are spread all over our land. The young adults are also enrolled in either "Apostolic or Youth" organizations while the children belong to the organization of the young knights. The father encourages and stays vigilant as he too belongs to the "Fraternity of the Immaculate Conception." These

Marian organizations, sororities and fraternities have spread among Maronite men and women over four hundred years.

The Maronite family willingly accepts everything that is related to the Virgin Mary, whether it has come from the East or from the West; whether it spoke Greek, Syriac, Italian or Persian!

This is how our families were able to preserve their faith in these valleys and mountains. This is how our ancestors lived for a long time, between the large church and the small church, i.e., the family. Their faith remained as strong as a rock. They have carried it to the ends of the earth where they are scattered throughout one hundred forty countries according to the most recent statistics. In whatever country the Maronite family lived, it carried along the icon of the Virgin Mary, gathered its children around it and chanted the hymn of *Ya Umm Allah* which is rendered "O Mother of God."

In spite of the harsh realities of the time when our families have either migrated or have been scattered or displaced; in spite of the challenges of today's world, the invention of motion picture, video and television; in spite of the work-frenzy world that never stops day or night, this is how our families, until today, have maintained the faith. Gradually, however, with this kind of world in which we live, the icon of the Virgin Mary began to disappear and her light began to dim! I am afraid that the light of faith may also have begun to dim and turn pale.

The pollutions of the city have contaminated the clear mountain skies. The densely populated areas have strangled the "altar of the Virgin Mary" in their tiny living quarters. Today's situation is turned around, the family is no longer under the protection of the parents where it gathered for prayer in the evening. This is why we reaffirm that saying: The icon of the Virgin Mary gathers, her prayers intercede and her light shines through the darkness of life. Quite often countless stories are told about the true reality that kept the faith of the Russian families alive after the Marxist Revolution; and that was the icon of the Virgin Mary in the house, a "soft light" in front of it, and a grandmother's singing without fear or hesitation.

We must not put out the "lighted lamp" which stands before the icon of the Virgin Mary. Let us maintain the tradition of our Christian families and secure in each one an "icon of the Virgin Mary," a "soft light" in front of it. Let us also salute her icon every morning and evening with a "Hail Mary," then for certain, she would continue to protect the faith in our families!

Many a family, individually and collectively, consecrate themselves to the Virgin Mary and pray to her! This has been a practice from antiquity. This is why we confirm some of the prayers that we have collected from the Church Fathers which may help us in our individual and communal prayer in front of her icon! Most of these prayers are commonly used and, for every event, they carry with them the cries and sighs of the centuries.

1. The Prayer of Saint Ephrem

This prayer is chosen from Saint Ephrem's commentary on the prophecy of Isaiah which says that the virgin will conceive and bear a Son who shall be called Emmanuel. It contains the appeal of Saint Ephrem, who is known as the Marian poet, and dates back to the middle of the fourth century:

> "O Mary, you are the safe harbor to the stranded; a mother to every orphan; a joy to the sick; a smile to the sorrowing. You are the Sun of the world and the pure hand that destroys the fetters. O Mary, you are always there for us. Amen."

2. The Prayer of Saint Rabbula of Edessa

Bishop Rabbula attended the Council of Ephesus in which the dogma of "Mary, Mother of God" was proclaimed in 431. He returned to his diocese urging the faithful to ask for Mary's intercession as he himself prayed before them this prayer upon his return from the council:

> "Hail Mary, you are the Ark of the Mysteries; Hail Mary, you are a blessed field; Hail Mary, you are a living banquet upon whom the faithful prepared the Bread of Life. Intercede always for us, we who, in all faithfulness, honor you in fitting praises...

Protect us, O Mother of God, under the mantle of your prayers and keep away from us all misfortunes for you are our refuge, our great hope and our revival. Put an end to all dissensions that are caused by our own sins, and grant us that peace which is truly yours, O Blessed Virgin Mary. Amen."

3. The Prayer of Saint Augustine

Saint Augustine was the bishop of Hippo, near Carthage, where some people were still praying in the Phoenician language. He most often beseeched the Virgin Mary in his sermons and urged his flock to be close to her and to ask for her intercession. This prayer dates back to the middle of the fifth century.

"... O Blessed Virgin Mary, the entire creation is at your feet weighing down under a painful slavery, to receive your mercy and to petition you to answer our request with the same "yes" you answered the Angel when he proposed to you...! O glorious Mary, who can offer the thanksgiving due to you for the generous help you have bestowed upon this afflicted world. What praise could our weak human nature offer you when, at the brink of being lost and in despair, it found in you the dawn of its salvation. Then, be merciful and accept the gratitude of our weak nature, because no matter how great it may be, it does not even measure up to what you deserve. Answer our prayers, reconcile us to God, petition for us the pardon of our sins, we ask this as we depend on your intercession. Confer upon us the graces necessary for our salvation and accept our offering for you are the only hope for sinners. Through you, we ask for the forgiveness of our sins and wait to receive the reward for our good deeds.

O Holy Mary, sustain the poor, safeguard the fearful, strengthen the weak, pray for the people, intercede on behalf of the clergy, petition for women, and make all who celebrate your memory recognize the work of your

mercy. Look with compassion toward those who take
refuge under your protection and grant their requests.
O Blessed Virgin, pray constantly to God for the sake of
the faithful, you who deserved to carry the Savior of the
world, who lives and reigns forever and ever. Amen."

4. **The Prayer of Saint John Damascene**

After helping his father who worked for the Umayyads in
Damascus, he entered the monastery and dedicated his life to
prayer, meditation and writing. The best of what was written
about the Assumption of the Virgin Mary into Heaven, body
and soul, was penned by the "Damascene." This seventh
century meditation is a perfect example:

> "We stand before you today, O Holy Queen, yes I
> repeat, the Queen, the Virgin Mother of God: We place
> our hope in you as if it is fastened to a sure and firm
> anchor (Hebrews 6:19) we dedicate to you our mind,
> our soul and our body, each one of us entirely: as we
> honor you with "psalms, praises and spiritual hymns"
> (Ephesians 5:19 and Colossians 3:16) as much as we
> possibly can, because honoring you according to your
> rank is far beyond our capability. Those who keep your
> memorial in holiness would be satisfied to receive the
> gift of your immeasurable mercy, since it is for them
> the climax of everlasting joy. What Blessedness or
> Goodness does not fill with grace those who make of
> their mind the hidden dwelling place of your sacred
> memory!
>
> This is a proof of the appreciation and the attempt of
> our simple mind, which had forgotten its personal
> weakness, when it was revived by your love. O highly
> exalted Queen, Mother of our merciful Lord, watch over
> us. Design our destiny according to your will. Guide our
> journey toward the safe haven of the Divine Will; grace
> us with the eternal joy—the bright Light which shines
> from the face of God the Word himself—who took flesh
> from you. To Him, to the Father and to the merciful

and life-giving Holy Spirit, we offer glory, honor and power now, at all times, and forever and ever. Amen.

5. In the Shadow of your Protection

This old prayer was found in a Greek manuscript from either the fourth or the fifth century. It is known among Christians both in the East and the West where the old text reads as follows:

> "O Mother of God, we take refuge in the shadow of your protection. Do not permit that anyone who seeks your intercession fall into temptation. But deliver us from danger, O you, who alone are pure, O you, who alone are blessed. Amen."

The more recent prayer is as follows:

> In the shadow of your protection we take refuge, O most gracious Mother of God. Do not despise our petitions when we come to you in need, but deliver us from danger, O Mary, you who are glorified and blessed. Amen.

CONCLUSION

As we conclude this Marian Procession which brings us from the Old Testament to the New Testament, to the Church Fathers, to the Ecumenical Councils, to the prayers, to the "Paraliturgical devotions and the Qurbono," we have reached the "Harbor!" Should we rest here?

By no means! We must continue our journey now that we are at the threshold of the third Christian millennium. In the encyclical *Redemptoris Mater* or "Mother of the Redeemer," Pope John Paul II invited the Church to continue the "Journey" of history with Mary who still occupies the "highest rank" among the people of God, "because, from now on, she is the fulfillment of the Church on the last day." Therefore, "the Church reaches its perfection through the person of the Blessed Virgin Mary."

The purpose of this journey is to reveal the face of the Virgin Mary in a struggling Church who upholds her at a very high regard in every heart, home and shrine. May these pages serve as a beginning study and meditation, because our attempt was neither to conduct an extensive research nor to delve into the depth of this topic. But we intended it to provide a helping guide to assist those who wish to enter the Marian revelation within the Maronite Church.

I should hope that I have paid my debt toward Our Blessed Mother, because near the Church of "Our Lady" I was born; from her baptismal font I received the Chrism and the faith; around her lectern I prayed and upon her altar I celebrated my first *Qurbono*. In Cyprus also, my Cathedral was named after Our Lady.

If I were to have a wish for our people who have been scattered all over the world during these trying times, it would be to repeat the saying of the Patriarch Elias El-Houwayek, when he dedicated in 1908 the Shrine of Our Lady of Lebanon in Harissa:

> "Yes the storms hang over our heads, but the Virgin Mary who protected this Mountain until today, she will continue to protect it. Just like in battle, as the soldiers exchange the password lest they fall in the enemy's hand, so should we exchange the password of hope which is: 'the Virgin Mary'. "

To practice these wishes we suggest the following:

1. Marian Shrines are Places of Prayer and Worship

We should do the impossible to keep our Marian shrines: Harissa, Ileej, Qannoubeen and the rest..., as true places of pilgrimage and prayer in which we renew our faith. We must facilitate and put at the service of our people all modern amenities, so they may be able to visit these shrines, pray, repent and meditate. Let everything be at their disposal: the churches, the manpower and the monetary means. We must employ modern technology to help make each shrine a "Cana of Galilee" whereby the water would be changed into wine and where we would hear Mary say: "Do whatever He tells you."

2. Parish Churches are the Meeting Place of the Community

The church is the house of God and the house of the people; that is where people encounter God. Let our churches and liturgical services be as such. If the Liturgy dies, then "God dies" within the heart of the community. In Church we meet Jesus and His Mother year around. Therefore, let us live our liturgy in its complete cycle, let us diversify our prayers, prepare our celebrations and make of "Our Liturgy" not routine and boring meetings which people dread, but rather a "beautiful piece of art" adorned with artistic beauty and spiritual depth in which people would enthusiastically participate.

3. The Parish Churches and the Monasteries are Learning Centers

It is not enough for the parish church and the Monastery to be only a place for Liturgy, but they should have classrooms to serve as centers of learning and knowledge. "In the beginning was the Word!" Our people are thirsty to learn about their history, origins, spiritual and religious heritage. Let us put in their hands the methods and keys of learning. The "Scripture" is that key. Let the priest and the monk be the "teacher," the spiritual director and the facilitator, because the school is the introduction to the Church, and knowledge is the actual entrance into the journey of God's people. Let it be now as it was in Nazareth, where the children will grow in wisdom, knowledge and age before God and man.

4. Authentic Religious Art

Religious art is a part of God's beauty and creation. Maronite art is present in its history: the music, the singing, the iconography, the architecture, the furniture, the lighting, the decoration, the sound, the liturgical vestments..., all of these create conducive environment for prayer, meditation and encounter with God and the community. Why neglect this Tradition or leave it only to a small minority? It should be promoted and communicated to all churches, taught to our children and practiced today, not tomorrow, because we may wake up, some day, to find our churches empty and depleted especially of its vital power and resources.

5. The "Marian Youth"

The Youth are the future and the life of the Church; in fact, they are the Church of the third millennium. Our young people are typically Marian by nature and they spread all over our parishes. They should be our greatest concern and our continued interest. We must lead them to "verdant pasture," i.e., the Scripture! We ought to introduce them to the writing of the Church Fathers and to the authentic spiritual tradition. We need to be vigilant and attentive so as to watch over them because they may be lost before they join the "Legion of Mary" or enroll in "Apostolic Organizations" which truly can change the face of the world.

6. The "Icon of Mary, the Mother of God"

Whether at home or in church we must return to the original icon where Mary, the Mother of God, is present. Let us put aside our statues and cast our foreign paintings into art museums. But the icon of the Virgin Mary, modeled after the art of Rabbula and Ileej, must return to its place in the Church, in front of the railings, along with an oil lamp and the candles of the faithful. This way, the faithful may come to her at any time to whisper their anguish, to profess their faith and to be blessed as they present their concerns to God.

7. The Home—The Church

Our homes are consecrated to God and our families are the true "Temples of God." The home must have its privacy and the Christian family must have its serenity and peace. Let the "icon" of the Virgin Mary be on every face and in every home. Let there be an "Altar" for the Virgin Mary adorned with flowers, lights, incense and have on it our prayer-book and the Book of the Gospel. Let old and young greet Mary every day and night, every morning and evening. "Let each one of us take her home" as the Lord has instructed; and as John did, because her memory is sweet and her name is pure, she who deserves the most honorable greeting. Amen.

ARABIC SOURCES

The following is a list of some Arabic sources about the Blessed Virgin Mary in general and the Maronite Church in particular:

Al-Samrani, Reverend Philip. *The Month of Mary.* Beirut, 1981.

Beshara, Reverend Youssef, and Feghali, Reverend Paul. *The Virgin Mary.* Beirut, Clergy League Publications, 1979.

Bistany, Karam. *Queen of Virgins.* Beirut, Catholic Press, 1959.

Candella, Reverend Francis, S.J., *The Life of Mary, Mother of Jesus.* Beirut, Catholic Press, 1949.

Daou, Reverend Boutros. *Iconography of the Maronite Church: The Gospel of Rabbula and its Icons, The History of the Maronites, Volume VII.* Jounieh, St. Paul Press, 1987.

Daou, Reverend Boutros. *The Churches of Mary and the Maronites, The History of the Maronites, Volume VIII.* Jounieh, St. Paul Press, 1988.

Farah, Reverend Gabriel. *Mary, the Mother of Jesus.* Jounieh, St. Paul Press, 1970.

Gemayel, Reverend Boutros. *Prayer of the Faithful,* Three Volumes. Beirut, Catholic Press, 1966-1967.

Hobeika, Chorbishop Boutros. *The Virgin Mary is truly the Mother of God.* Research in this dogma as it stands in the Eastern Syriac

Church. Testimonials of the Divine Office in the Maronite Syriac Church. Beirut, Catholic Press, 1932.

Holy Spirit University Publications. *The Month of May*. Jounieh, 1987.

Khalifi, Bishop Abdou. *The Virgin Mary and the Issues of the Time*. Beirut, Dar Al-Mashriq Press, 1986.

Khashan, Reverend Youssef. *The Divine Treasure*. Jounieh, The Holy Spirit University Publications, 1984.

Nobert, Reverend. *Mary and Our Priesthood* (translated into Arabic by Father George Al-Mardini). Beirut, Clergy League Publications, 1985.

Pope Paul VI. *Apostolic Exhortation About Our Devotion to Mary*. Rome, 1974.

Pope John Paul II. The Encyclical *"Redemptoris Mater" or "Mother of the Redeemer."* Rome, 1987.

Sfeir, Patriarch Nasrallah Peter. Apostolic Letter on the occasion of the Marian Year, *About the Blessed Virgin Mary*. Jounieh, 1987.

Tarboush, Jamil. *The New Eve:* the series of "The Yeast in the Dough." Beirut, Catholic Press, 1967.

Tarboush, Jamil. *The Virtue of the Virgin Mary:* the series of "The Yeast in the Dough." Beirut, Catholic Press, 1967.

Thurian, Max. *Mary, the Mother of the Lord and the Symbol of the Church:* Theological Studies, (translated into Arabic by Khalil Rustum). Beirut, Dar Al-Mashriq Press, 1987.

An anonymous faithful devoted to Mary. *Mary Our Mother*. Beirut, Dakkash Press, 1983.

MARIAN BIBLIOGRAPHY

This list of Marian bibliography is adapted, just as it did appear in the Arabic Edition, with its Western languages: English, French and Italian.

Hobeika, J. et P. *Titres de la Tres Sainte Vierge Marie d'après le breviaire et les offices divins.* Hadath—Beyrouth, 1903. (Arabe, Francais, Syriaque).

Hobeika, J. et P. *Temoignage de L'eglise syro-maronite en faveur de L'Immaculee Conception.* Hadath—Beyrouth, 1904.

Hobeika, J. et P. *Temoignage de L'eglise syro-maronite en faveur de L'Assomption de la Sainte Vierge.* Hadat—Beyrouth, 1925.

Maria, *Etudes sur la Sainte Vierge, sous la direction d'Hubert du Manoir.* Beauchesne, Paris, 1949 (t. I, t. II,).

Doumith, M., *"Marie dans la liturgie syro-maronite."* Maria, (t. I, pp. 327-340).

Goudard, J., *La Sainte Vierge au Liban.* Paris, 1908.

Jalabert, H., *La Sainte Vierge au Liban.* (seconde edition entierement refondue). Imprimerie Catholique, Beyrouth, 1953 (Trad. Anglaise).

Nasrallah, J., *Marie dans la sainte et divine liturgie byzantine.* Nouvelle Editions Latines. Paris, 1955.

Nasrallah, J., *le culte de Marie en Orient.* Paris. 1971.

Evdokimov, P., *L'art de L'Icone.* Desclee de Brouwer, 1972.

Le Pape Paul VI, *Le culte Marial.* 1974.

Zayek, Francis, *Mary, Cedar of Our Catholic Faith.* Detroit, 1975.

Thurian, Max, *Marie, Mere du Seigneur, Figure de L'eglise.* Edition du Cerf, 1983.

Moubarak, Y., *Pentalogie antiochienne.* Cenacle Libanais, 1984, (t. III, pp. 479-495).

Sader, Y., *Peinture Murales dans les eglises maronite Medievales.* Beyrouth, 1987.

Le Pape Jean-Paul II, L'encyclique *"Redemptoris Mater."* Roma, 1987.

Congregazion per il culto divino, *Orientamenti e proposte Per l'anno Mariano.* Roma, 1987.

Congregazione per le chiese orientali, *L'enciclica "Redemptoris Mater" e le chiese orientali nell' anno mariano.* Roma, 1987.

Glossary and Translation
of Aramaic Terms

Throughout the text, only Arabic footnotes and bibliography are translated into English. The footnotes and bibliography written in English, French or Italian, are left in their respective languages. Some Aramaic terms are translated others are defined in order to facilitate the reading process. Those terms are italicized throughout the text. They may be names like *Ephrem*, or book titles like *Sheheemto* or *Fenqitho,* or adjectives like *Olmo,* or liturgical services like *Zuyoho* and *Qurbono,* or prayers and hymns like *Hoosoyo* and *Qolo.* However, Arabic terms originating in Syriac such as *Ephremiat, Ya'coubiat* or the like, are explained in the text where they actually occur.

Anaphora of Sharrar: *Anaphora* means offerings or gifts and constitutes the second major part of the Mass, whereas the Liturgy of the Word constitutes the first, which ends with the homily. *Sharrar* means confirmation or to confirm. In the text, the expression refers to the oldest Maronite Eucharistic Prayer known as the "*Anaphora* of the Apostles." This particular *Anaphora* is also found in the Eastern Syriac Tradition.

Ephrem (303-373): Born in Nisibis, Mesopotamia, he is one of the most prolific writers among the Fathers of the Syriac Church. His famous commentary on the *Diatessaron* and his extensive theological treaties in prose are just as impressive as his countless hymns in poetry. His composition of metrical verses, which dominated the Syriac liturgical tradition, made him one of the greatest poets of the Universal Church. Although he was declared Doctor of the Universal Church by Pope Benedict XV as recently as 1920, he has always been considered the Teacher, the Deacon and the "Harp of the Holy Spirit" in the Syriac Church. His talents and eloquence, from a very young age earned him a rare reputation for being a gifted commentator, orator, poet, teacher and defender of the faith. He is said to have accompanied Bishop Jacob to the Council of Nicaea in 325. His feast day falls on January 28.

Fenqitho: Means "volume, book or collection of feasts." In the texts it refers to the collection of various liturgical texts expressing the theme of the feast day. It was originally published in Rome in two volumes: the winter *Fenqitho* in 1656, and the summer *Fenqitho* in 1666. Be they the feast days of the Lord, the Virgin Mary or the Saints, they are coordinated with the Maronite Liturgical Calendar. It is also called the "Sanctoral Cycle."

Hoosoyo: The *Hoosoyo* is the highlight of the *Qurbono* and expresses the liturgical theme of the feast or the day. It is a unique type of prayer which offers a scriptural interpretation along with a series of supplications petitioning God's protection and forgiveness. It consists of four parts: *Proemion, Sedro, Qolo* and *Etro*.

- The ***Proemion*** is the introductory prayer, which offers praise, worship and magnificent titles to Christ, and in some different feast days, to the Trinity.
- The ***Sedro*** constitutes the heart of the *Hoosoyo* and through its catechetical function it reflects the theme of the particular Sunday or the feast day being celebrated. It further presents, in a litany form, petitions asking for the Lord's assistance. It is poetic in nature and is composed of several strophes in metric form.
- The ***Qolo*** is a response to the series of supplications whereby it magnifies the theme of the *Hoosoyo* and accentuates its character.
- ***Etro*** means sweet perfume (of incense) and is the conclusion of the *Hoosoyo*. It summarizes the petitions of the Church who asks God to accept its precious offering which is consumed and raised to the heights. The burning of incense is par excellence an act of purification.

Ho Qteelo Bmesren: The expression means: there is the (Paschal Lamb) slain in Egypt. In the text, it refers to a special hymn replicated after the familiar hymn of *Ya Sha'bee Wa Sahbee* which means "O my People, O my Friends."

Korozooto: Is a diaconal proclamation following the Gospel. It reflects the theme of the Word of God for that particular Sunday and announces the homily.

Olmo: Means virgin. In the text, it refers to the virgin about whom Isaiah prophesied.

Qolo: Means a poetic hymn sung with its particular tune. See above.
Qolo Fsheeto: Refers to a poetic type of hymn which is composed with hepta-syllabic measure. It is also a hymn used with alternate verses of another hymn or psalm.

Qoom Faoulos: *Qoom,* by itself means position, rising, standing; it refers to a station or a watch of the night. *Faoulos* means Paul. In the text it refers to a designated type of a hymn for these stations. The hymn may be attributed to Saint Paul the Apostle.

Qurbono: Means offering, oblation or Eucharist. Throughout the text, the term refers to the Mass or the Service of the Holy Mysteries.

Qadeesho: Means holy, saintly and pure. It also refers to a Saint or a holy person. Thus, the Arabic term *"Qadeesha"* which refers to the "Holy Valley" located in Northern Lebanon and served as a refuge for monks, hermits, saintly people and patriarchs during times of persecution.

Reesh Qurian: Or *Foorish Qurian,* is a collection of readings selected from the Scriptures according to the Maronite Syriac Liturgical Year in manuscript form. The oldest collection dates to 1242. The most recent was published in 1841, in the monastery of Saint Anthony, *Quzhaya,* located in the *Qadeesha* valley.

Sheheemto: Is the book of the Divine Office or the Prayer of the Hours, which covers the entire Liturgical Year according to the Maronite Syriac Antiochene Church. It was printed in Rome for the first time in 1624. However, many subsequent editions followed in 1877, 1885 and 1938, just to name a few.

Sooghito: Is a hymn of petitions or supplications. In the *Qurbono*, the supplications are interchangeable with the *Qolo* (see *Hoosoyo*) which precedes the *Etro*. However, in the Divine Office, the list of petitions is much longer and it is situated between the Readings and the concluding prayer.

Sooghyoto: Is the plural of *Sooghito*.

Teshmeshto: Means service, rite, ministry, office or worship. In the text, it refers to the liturgical books that contain the texts of the holy days of obligations and the memorials. The majority of these books are still in manuscript form.

Zuyoho: Means procession. Thus the Arabic term *Ziyah*. In the text, it refers to the Procession or the paraliturgical devotional service.

Christotokos: Is a Greek word meaning "Mother of Christ."

Theotokos: Is a Greek term for "Mother of God" and literally means "God-bearer."

Personal Reflections

Personal Reflections

Personal Reflections

Personal Reflections

Printed by Delft Printing, Inc. www.delftprinting.com